An Introduction to the Writings

of Saint Teresa

AN INTRODUCTION
TO THE
WRITINGS OF SAINT TERESA

Sebastian V. Ramge, O.C.D.

HENRY REGNERY COMPANY   CHICAGO 1963

Nihil obstat quominus imprimatur:

Rev. John Clarke, O.C.D.
Rev. Christopher Latimer, O.C.D.

Imprimi potest:

Holy Hill, Wisconsin
January 31, 1963
Very Rev. Christopher Latimer, O.C.D. Provincial

Imprimatur:

Rt. Rev. Msgr. George J. Casey
Vicar General
April 23, 1963

The Nihil obstat and Imprimatur are official declarations that a book or pamphlet is free of doctrinal or moral error. No implication is contained therein that those who have granted the Nihil obstat and Imprimatur agree with the contents, opinions, or statements expressed.

To a world ruled by power she opposed her inner world, conquered in powerless rapture and ruled by self-deposition. Complete self-deposition was the foundation of her true kingdom of God.

René Fülöp-Miller

ACKNOWLEDGEMENTS

The foundation upon which I have constructed this book is the course on Saint Teresa given by Father Thomas of the Cross, O.C.D. in the Institute of Spirituality conducted by the Discalced Carmelite Fathers in Rome. I am grateful to him for his graciousness in permitting me to do this. The bibliography found in the last chapter is mainly the work of Father Otilio of the Child Jesus, O.C.D., a Teresian scholar of long standing. His generosity with the bibliography is an eloquent testimony to his ardent desire of having Teresa known and loved. To the students upon whom I experimented by giving this course a hearty "thank you." I am also indebted to a very patient and gracious typist, Miss Susan Shy. Last, but not least, I wish to express my gratitude to those who encouraged me in the writing of this brief guide.

TABLE OF CONTENTS

An Introduction to the Writings

of Saint Teresa

CHAPTER ONE

On Eagle's Wings

THE WARM brightness of the Spanish sun poured through the tall colorful windows. Polished sword-hilts and sparkling jewels glittered gaily in its light. Somber academic gowns and modest friars' robes lost their reserve in the many-hued reflections of the windows. The ancient hall buzzed with excitement.

Never had the University of Salamanca witnessed a similar occurrence. Mother Teresa of Jesus, canonized only a few years before in 1622, was about to receive the hat and gown of a *doctor of theology.* "Women should be silent in the churches" Saint Paul admonished, and so it was impossible for Teresa to be declared a *doctor of the Church.* Her countrymen, the professors and students of the university, however, voted to award her with as much as they could, so Teresa would receive recognition for her profound writings. It was a gala afternoon, one burned into the history of this great university.

And, indeed, seldom in Church history has there been a more eminently catholic figure than St. Teresa. To this day whoever desires to know the spirit of Catholicism needs only to read her works. Written in obedience to superiors but with great personal reluctance these books have piloted countless souls on the way to perfection. For some, Teresa's writings have even opened the door to conversion as they did for Dr. Edith Stein, the renowned Jewish disciple of the philosopher Husserl. So greatly did these writings influence Miss Stein that she became a nun in Teresa's own Order and died a martyr for her people in the gas chambers of Auschwitz.

To know Teresa, and the only way we can know her is through her works, is to love her. She is as charming today as she was four centuries ago. Through the verve of her strong personality she influenced, not only close associates and acquaintances, but even persons of the highest religious, political, and intellectual rank. The formidable Philip II of Spain, for example, received Teresa's respectful but firm letters, and counted it an honor to heed her requests. On one occasion they actually met.[1]

The secret of St. Teresa's charm as an author lies in her disarming simplicity. In the works of Saint Teresa no pedantry or artificiality appears. Teresa expressed her thoughts as they occurred to her, without any desire to impress. She had a message to deliver; all else had to serve this end. No one hated affectation more than she; no one had a greater love for truth. She once remarked that, should a novice be found untruthful, she must be dismissed at once without regret. Describing a favor which the Lord granted her the Saint commented: "Thus I understood what it is for a soul to be walking in truth in the presence of Truth Itself." Earlier she had remarked: "It gave me a very great desire to speak only of things which are very true and which go far beyond any that are treated of in the world."[2]

For Teresa, truth and humility were inseparable sisters. "To be humble is to walk in truth, for it is absolutely true to say that we have no good thing in ourselves, but only misery and nothingness; and any-

1. *The Letters of St. Teresa of Jesus* (Letter 195a) addressed to Doña Inés Nieto, I, 484.
2. *Autobiography*, chap. xl.

one who fails to understand this is walking in false-hood. He who best understands it is most pleasing to Sovereign Truth because he is walking in truth."[3]

Her esteem for these two virtues made Teresa genu-inely *herself*. Veracity of this type points to solid ma-turity for, according to psychiatrists, the heart of maturity is the acceptance of the truth of one's own self with its lights and its shadows and the eventual development of one's latent potentialities. Through her writings the reader receives a distinct impression of Teresa's personality, and he feels that he knows her very well indeed. He knows of her foibles, her mis-takes; he observes her progress in conquering her limitations; he discovers the virtues Teresa would hide from him.

Gratitude, Aesop's "sign of noble souls," ranked high in Teresa's personal ethics. Excessive though it might have seemed at times, her sense of gratitude fit into the general pattern of her personality. Teresa was not a woman to tolerate half-measures or slipshod decisions; a thing either was or was not, it was to be done or it was to be left alone. When she thanked a person for his generosity, she meant it. "I admit that

3. *Interior Castle*, VI Mansion, chap. x.

4

my sense of gratitude is not a perfection—it comes too naturally to me. I think that I could be bribed with a sardine!"

People sometimes falsely conclude that cloistered nuns have to be misanthropes to survive within the confines of convent walls. Teresa of Avila confutes this line of reasoning for she loved people and wanted them to love her. Whoever met her immediately felt at ease in her presence. Before Teresa realized that dedicating one's life to God means a great deal more than sitting in the convent parlor indulging in spiritual conversations for the supposed good of souls, the sophisticates of Avila thought it quite the fashion to go to the convent parlor to chat with this witty nun. Teresa was surprised to see a very stern Christ standing before her as she was absorbed one day in a conversation which was more frivolous than spiritual. "It made such an impression on me that, although it is now more than twenty-six years ago, I seem to have Him present with me still. I was greatly astonished and upset about it, and I never wanted to see that person again."[4]

Had Teresa not given her life to God through the

4. *Autobiography,* chap. vii.

vows of religion, she would have undoubtedly been one of the most outstanding social figures of her era. Catherine of Aragon, Catherine de Medici, Mary Queen of Scots, Mary Tudor and Elizabeth I were all contemporary with her, but Teresa easily outshines all of them. She was as much at ease with high-ranking nobility as she was with the coarse muleteers who transported her and her nuns from one foundation to another. She was very amiable, and a single visit with her was sufficient to convert an adversary to her way of thinking—and with a great deal of enthusiasm as well.

Father Bartholomew de Medina, a Dominican professor at the University of Salamanca, was strongly prejudiced against Teresa. He was very cautious in his dealings with her and a few times he inveighed against her in the presence of his students. Teresa determined to win his approval and tried a little innocent bribery. From Alba de Tormes she sent to the prioress of the Carmelite convent in Salamanca a freshly caught trout with the following note: "The trout which accompanies this letter was sent me today by the Duchess. I thought it such a fine one that I have got this messenger to send it to my father, Master Fray Bartholomew de Medina. If it arrives before dinner, will Your Reverence send it to him at once by Miguel, and also the enclosed letter? If it comes later, do not fail to send it to him just the same, and we shall see if he will write me a few lines."[5] Father de Medina quickly became one of Teresa's greatest admirers!

She was irresistible. "People have such a blind confidence in me—I don't know how they can do such things, but they seem to trust me so implicitly that they will give me as much as a thousand or two thousand ducats," Teresa wrote to her brother Lorenzo.[6]

Despite the passage of four centuries the humanity of this Saint still vibrates on every page of her books. At times she can comment on her feminine vanity: "If the medallion had come in the days when I wore gold ornaments I should have coveted it dreadfully, for it is extremely pretty."[7] She can express her gratitude in such an attractive manner that she seems to invite further benefits: "The butter was delicious, as I should have expected it to be, coming from you, and

5. *The Letters of St. Teresa of Jesus* (Letter 51) addressed to Mother Anne of the Incarnation, I, 130.
6. *The Letters of St. Teresa of Jesus* (Letter 19) addressed to Lorenzo de Cepeda, I, 75.
7. *The Letters of St. Teresa of Jesus* (Letter 2) addressed to Lorenzo de Cepeda, I, 34.

as everything is that you send me. I shall accept it in the hope that, when you have any more nice butter, you will remember me again, for it does me a lot of good. The quince cheese was delicious too; really, you seem to be thinking of nothing but making me happy."[8]

Her humor and wit are proverbial. A new convent was plagued with lice; Teresa decided to take a hand in ridding the convent of the pests. She organized the mystified nuns into a procession and had them walk through the halls chanting a little poem of her composition:

> Since Thou giv'st us, King of Heaven,
> New Clothes like these—
> Do Thou keep nasty creatures
> Out of this frieze!

Not many laughed at or teased Saint John of the Cross—Teresa did. Roguishly, she begged deliverance from these who try to make everyone into perfect contemplatives.

Personality and spirituality are mutually related. One cannot be understood without the other. Sanctity is spiritual maturity, an impossibility without the hu-

8. *The Letters of St. Teresa of Jesus* (Letter 23) addressed to Doña Catalina Hurtado, I, 81.

man maturity of the person. In other words, sanctity is "wholeness" and denotes an integral human being. To understand a saint, the use of historical and psychological analyses are disappointing; instead, the saint must be contemplated in the light of theology. The lives of God's servants reflect a healthy collusion between divine grace and human docility under the direction of supernatural ideals.

A saint is not a bizarre eccentric. He differs from the "standard" Christian only in intensity, a fullness engendered by a profound comprehension of his vocation as a member of the Mystical Body of Christ. He embodies in his finite being the doctrine and example of Christ.

Little is known of the life of Christ, for a mysterious silence has thrown a veil over much of it. Ambitious studies attempt to penetrate the personality of the Incarnate Word;[9] they base themselves upon available scriptural data supplemented by the physiological evidence present on the Shroud of Turin, but the sparsity of information leaves much to be desired. Perhaps

9. Alejandro Roldan, S.J., *Introducción a la Ascética Diferencial* (Madrid: Editorial Razón y Fe, 1960); and various references in René le Senne, "Traité de Caracterologie," *PUF,* (1952).

Divine Providence willed this to permit each to adapt the universal example of Christ to his circumstances and needs according to the psychological, cultural, social, and intellectual environment in which he finds himself. God has no need of slaves in His service—He has called His followers "friends."

Divine grace does not replace human nature, but it does perfect it. The spiritual life, born at baptism through reception of sanctifying grace, is destined to fill the abyss man has dug between himself and his Creator through his dismal felony in the garden of Eden. Its expansion is possible only through the activity of the virtues: *theological,* intended to unite man directly with God, and *moral,* intended to perfect human activity. Later, the inspiration of the Holy Ghost (through the operation of *the seven gifts*) leads the soul to integral spiritual maturity. But the foundation of this entire edifice, the basis of one's imitation of Christ, is the virtue of Faith.

Teresa of Avila, despite her great activity in establishing convents and monasteries and despite the excellent books she wrote, rejoiced in her last moments because she was dying "a daughter of the Church." She ascended to sublime heights of Christian maturity, but she confessed that her favorite reading was the catechism and she heartily recommended it to all. However rich her friendship with God, she never lost her simplicity.

Beyond the personal acceptance of Faith and its complete integration into her thought and activity, Teresa of Jesus went a step further toward sanctity by accepting Christ. At first glance, this seems a logical consequence of Faith, and so it is, but the amazing fact remains that not every "Christ-ian" has wholeheartedly accepted Him. Many Christians are content to hold to the dogmas taught them by Church authority and to fulfill their obligations. But the conviction that Faith means more, that it is personalized in Jesus Christ—this escapes them. Acceptance of the Lord implies a definite commitment to His divine and human Person. In this atmosphere Faith develops and the virtues of Hope and Charity come into focus.

Teresa's unwitting testimony to her personal embodiment of Faith through committing herself to Christ can be found in her motives for inaugurating the first convent of the strict Camelite observance in Avila: "And, seeing that I was a woman and a sinner, and incapable of doing all that I should like in the Lord's service, and that my whole yearning was, and still is, that, as He has so many enemies and so few

11

friends, these last should be trusty ones, I determined to do the little that was in me. . . ."[10] Teresa decided, therefore, that she would serve Christ by offering generous souls the opportunity of dedicating themselves *completely* to His service. Through this dedication these souls, under Teresa's leadership as foundress, would grow in love of the object of Christ's love (the Church) and His interests would become theirs. This decision demanded courage, for, in addition to the limitations imposed by her sex, Teresa had to face the city fathers' violent opposition to a new convent. "All this made such a commotion in the city that people talked about nothing else. Everybody was condemning me and going to see the Provincial and visiting my convent. I was no more distressed by all they were saying about me than I should have been if they had said nothing at all, but I was afraid that the foundation might be dissolved, and that distressed me a great deal. . . ."[11]

Teresa knew more than one bitter struggle during her life, but it is remarkable how calm she remained despite them. Her secret, of course, was her great love of Christ and her awareness that He loved her. "He

10. *Way of Perfection,* chap. i.
11. *Autobiography,* chap. xxxvi.

who truly loves Thee, my God, travels by a broad and a royal road and travels securely. It is far away from any precipice, and hardly has such a man stumbled in the slightest degree when Thou, Lord, givest him Thy hand . . . Our eyes must be fixed upon Him and we must not be afraid that this Sun of Justice will set, or that He will allow us to travel by night and so be lost, unless we first forsake Him."[12]

Teresa grieved over the dishonor heretics gave to God by failing to actualize the endowments He showered upon them. "There came to my notice the harm and havoc that were being wrought in France by these Lutherans and the way in which their unhappy sect was increasing. This troubled me very much and, as though I could do anything, or be of any help in the matter, I wept before the Lord and entreated Him to remedy this great evil. . . . What has become of Christians now? Must those who owe Thee most always be those who distress Thee most?"[13]

Love cannot be idle. No greater source of creativeness can be found than in true love. The saint's union with God is mirrored by the love between husband and wife. Just as the love of the spouses results in

12. *Autobiography,* chap. xxxv.
13. *Way of Perfection,* chap. i.

countless little manifestations of their love, so the love between God and the saint flowers in many acts of love. The life of Teresa of Jesus illustrates this perfectly. She was never content with half-measures— she was passionately dedicated to Christ and to His Church. The many fatiguing journeys, the many convents she founded, the unnumbered souls she helped— all these were the fruit of Teresa's love.

The glorious summit of a holy life is genuine heroism. If an incident of childhood can presage the future course of life, then the attempt of the young Teresa to run away into Moorish territory in quest of martyrdom serves as an eloquent index to her later heroism. Much later, at her canonization, it was said: a sickly woman, inflamed with a courageous love of Christ, sustained her ideal of offering generous individuals an opportunity for absolute dedication to Christ: that woman is Teresa of Jesus, foundress of the Discalced Carmelite Order and authoress of "treatises on mystical theology and other pious writings."[14]

In addition to its sanctifying activity within the individual, divine grace has ecclesiastical value also. Whatever might be his position in civil or religious

14. Pope Gregory XV, *Bull of Canonization*, March 12, 1622.

society, each member of the Mystical Body receives graces to fulfill a definite role in the Church to which he has been destined by divine wisdom. "As in one body we have many members, but all the members have not the same office: so we being many are one body in Christ, and every one members one of another."[15]

Teresa stands as one of God's answers to Martin Luther. The *Augsburg Confession,* a profession of faith drafted with Luther's assistance and approval in 1530 (when Teresa was fifteen), states that "men cannot be justified[16] before God by their own powers, merits, or works, but are justified freely for Christ's sake through faith, when they believe that they are received into favor . . . Man cannot prepare himself for God's activity by a deep sorrow, an earnest longing . . . Man is justified solely by faith." Luther denied the reality of interior grace and the reality of justification through interior grace; he even went so far as to say that man remains basically corrupt, for even after justification sin remains in the depths of the soul. The only saving quality about man is the fact

15. Romans xii, 4.
16. Justification—interior renewal by forgiveness of sin and integrity of life.

that God "covers over" human depravity in the faithful by applying the grace of Christ.

Saint Teresa of Jesus, by her life and writings, taught that man is regenerated by a complete inner renewal through the activity of grace; she further illustrated man's ability to grow to his full spiritual stature by cooperating with grace and by seeking to detach himself from even the slightest shadow of sin. To Luther's concept of man as basically bad as a consequence of original sin, Teresa unknowingly opposed her faith in the essential goodness of man. The historian Macaulay has written: "Saint Teresa contributed more to stemming the tide of Protestantism than did Philip II and Saint Ignatius Loyola." In another place, this same historian wrote: "If Ignatius of Loyola is the brain of the Catholic reaction, Teresa of Jesus is its heart; if Ignatius is the head of a great band, Teresa of Jesus belongs completely to its humanity."

Teresa's influence reaches far beyond the limits of her own century. Her role in the Mystical Body is a prominent one and her influence will be felt in the Church until the end of time. Teresa not only founded an Order whose main end is to increase devotion to the spiritual life, but she laid the foundation

of a universal school of spirituality. The wisdom of
Saint Teresa and her spiritual insights have inspired
theologians and religious psychologists and in the
course of time a definite interpretation of spirituality
in the light of her doctrine has been formulated. The
special merit of this "school" of spirituality is its
equilibrium in insisting upon both the speculative
theological and the practical psychological principles
of spirituality.

A great amount of testimony in support of Teresa's
authority could be produced from the writings of the
Supreme Pontiffs alone, but a quotation from Saint
Pius X seems adequate: "Whoever desires to lead a
life of holiness, let him study these (the writings of
St. Teresa) and he will have need of no others. For in
them this renowned mistress of piety points out a safe
path of Christian life from its inception up to the
consummation and perfection of virtue; she sets down
accurately the ways best suited for correcting vicious
habits, quelling boisterous passions, and effacing the
defilements of sin; and she puts before the reader
every enticement to virtue . . . As regards mystical
theology Teresa discourses about those higher re-
gions of the spiritual life with such ease that she
seems to be in her proper sphere . . . Yet she says not

17

one word which conflicts with exact Catholic theology . . . Whoever will reflect on these teachings of Saint Teresa will come to understand how deservedly writers on these difficult subjects have acknowledged her as a master and have followed her guidance and, furthermore, with what justice the Church prays God 'that we may be nourished by the food of her heavenly doctrine and instructed by the ardor of her tender piety.' Would that those who now write about what they call 'mystical psychology' would make up their minds to follow in the footsteps of this great mistress!"[17]

17. Pius X, "Letter for the Third Centenary of Teresa's Beatification," March 7, 1914.

CHAPTER TWO

The Language of Heaven

SIXTEENTH century Europe produced outstanding women: Catherine of Aragon, unhappy wife of the lecherous Henry VIII; Catherine de Medici, crafty instigator of the gruesome St. Bartholomew's Day massacre; Mary I Tudor, unfairly nicknamed "Bloody Mary"; Mary, the imprudent Queen of Scots; Elizabeth I, "Good Queen Bess"; and Marie de Medici, queen and regent of France. Teresa must have heard of all these contemporaries in her convent parlor, and perhaps the historical significance of their lives impressed Teresa. She certainly had been impressed by heroic Christian women: "There have been other women who have done heroic deeds for love of Thee. I myself am fit only to talk and, therefore, my God, it is not Thy good pleasure to test me by actions."[1]

1. *Autobiography,* chap. xxi.

But no one was greater than Teresa of Jesus herself. Only an extraordinarily courageous woman would dare to undertake the work Teresa did despite ill health and loud opposition; only a vigorous woman could dare demand of nuns: "I want you to be strong men. If you do all that is in you, the Lord will make you so manly that men themselves will be amazed at you."[2]

The sixteenth century queens are regarded either as historical personalities and studied by unemotional specialists or as the objects of sentimental attraction or "cult"; Teresa, however, is as vibrant, as dynamic, as persuasive four centuries after her death as she was when she walked the dusty roads of Spain. "Although among her contemporaries were many persons distinguished for their holiness of life and knowledge of things divine—so that that period might justly be called the golden age of Catholic Spain—it must be admitted that Teresa combined in herself the virtues and gifts of all that pious band whom she numbered among her intimate friends and advisers."[3]

Teresa's influence has reached modern times through two means: the friars and nuns of the Order

2. *Way of Perfection,* chap. vii.
3. Pius X, "Letter for the Third Centenary of Teresa's Beatification," March 7, 1914.

she founded and her writings. The history of the Discalced Carmelite Order founded by Saint Teresa is another study. We shall omit it here, although a careful examination of the spirit of the Order does contribute to a complete understanding of the Saint.

Teresa was not a trained theologian or psychologist; her competency in these fields resulted from study, observation, and an insatiable desire to learn from men skilled in these sciences. When she wrote, her ideas reflected her knowledge and her conviction at the time of writing. As the Saint's spirituality matured, the development reflected in her later writings. Some authors fail to realize this. As a result, they present a distorted interpretation of Teresa's doctrine. For example, some try to make the seven mansions of the soul (described by the Saint in *The Interior Castle*) fit within the four stages of prayer Teresa described under the metaphor of the "four waters" in her autobiography. The consequence is an unintended disfigurement of her meaning, monstrous in its effects because it denies the tremendous extent of Teresa's grasp of spiritual doctrine. Actually, more than ten years of continual spiritual evolution elapsed between the writing of the two books.

Two rules guide a correct approach to Teresa's writings: objectivity and attention. Teresa wrote with conviction; she did not worry about the niceties of a plush rhetoric. This quickly manifests itself when we read the headings she attached to the different chapters of her work. Her readers must remain objective. They must try to enter into her thought and avoid the temptation to interpret according to their own preconceived line of thought. While it is true that Teresa is orthodox in matters of Faith and Morals, a too generous application of either theological or philosophical principles leads to many conclusions Teresa never intended. Further, Teresa was a balanced person gifted with outstanding integrity; consequently what she wrote in one place she did not simply deny in another, despite the apparent contradictions.

With these basic ideas in mind we can proceed to a study of Teresa's psychological and spiritual preparation for her mission.

*   *   *

Within a psychological framework St. Teresa's life can be divided into two definite stages. In the earlier stage, we find her life dominated by emotions; in the later, and longer, period we find an increasing dominion of the intellectual faculties.

The first period of St. Teresa's life extended from 1515 until a date roughly established as 1536, the year in which Teresa entered the Incarnation Convent.

For the first sixteen years of her life Teresa, gifted with a lively imagination (despite her personal evaluation of this faculty), lived in a rhapsodic atmosphere of knightly courage and chivalrous heroism. These phantasies were quickened by her furtive reading of novels disapproved by her father because of their frivolity. His ascetic outlook upon life could not countenance such a waste of time; he thought that the time devoted to these novels could be far more profitably used. Other contributors to Teresa's daydreaming were the glowing accounts of martyrdom she both heard and read. For example, these accounts led her to attempt flight with her brother Rodrigo so that the silvery swords of the Mohammedans could obtain for them the crown of martyrdom.

Teresa's father became alarmed at her capers and enrolled her in an Avilese boarding-school in 1531. This wise move caused a definite break with the "dream-world" of valiant knights and nebulous martyrs. About this time two persons entered Teresa's life and each, in his own way, contributed to her de-

23

velopment: Doña Maria Brinceño, mistress of the students at the boarding-school, and Don Pedro de Cepeda, Teresa's uncle. Through her godly and profitable conversations Doña Maria won Teresa's loving admiration. Don Pedro, on the other hand, insisted that Teresa read to him various tracts of asceticism, the letters of Saint Jerome, and parts of the *Third Spiritual Alphabet* by Francis Osuña. Fortunately for Teresa, Don Pedro's manly bearing and his solid reading matter balanced the somewhat sentimental nature of Teresa's attachment to Doña Maria.

Teresa entered the Carmelite Order in 1536. Her description of this event betrays an emotional confusion resulting from a conflict betwen emotion and reason. We must note this because it marks an important step in the progressive evolution of the Saint's maturity. "I had a close friend in another convent[4] and this gave me the idea that, if I was to be a nun, I would go only to the house where she was. I thought more about the pleasures of sense and vanity than of my soul's profit. . . . The Lord sent me a serious illness . . . I began to fear that, if I had died of my illness, I should have gone to hell; and though, even then, I

4. Teresa was referring to the Carmelite convent of the Incarnation in Avila.

could not incline my will to being a nun, I saw that this was the best and safest state, and so, little by little, I determined to force myself to embrace it . . . I used to try to convince myself by using the following argument. The trials and distresses of being a nun could not be greater than those of purgatory and I had fully deserved to be in hell. . . ."[5]

Gradually logic and solid reasoning deepened Teresa's formation of her objectives; she slowly learned to subject her emotional life to the influence of well-conceived principles. The change was difficult for a person as intensely emotional as Teresa, and she suffered from a temporary nervous disorder as a result. Also, several deaths in Teresa's immediate family forced her to reflect upon the passing nature of this life: in 1538 the death of her brother Rodrigo in Paraguay, the pious death of her father in 1544, the death of her brother Anthony in the battle of Inaquito in 1546.

Leonor de Mascarenhas, a Portuguese noblewoman who served as governess to King Philip II and to his ill-fated son Don Carlos, was a friend of Teresa's, and it very likely was she who gave the Saint the latest

5. *Autobiography,* chaps. iii and iv.

translation of Saint Augustine's *Confessions*. This was around 1554. The book had a powerful effect upon her, and, coupled with the spiritual direction of the Jesuit Fathers in Avila, it finally established Teresa firmly upon the path to psychological maturity.

The remaining years of Teresa's life furnish abundant proof of maturity. Aside from the equilibrium obvious in her writings there is the historical fact that she established sixteen convents, prepared the way for fourteen others, personally participated in the foundation of three others, and encouraged or inspired six more. A total of thirty-nine new convents—a fantastic record possible only where there is genuine psychological health. Within ten years after the inauguration of the "Reform" among the friars, Teresa could point out with maternal pride that there were more than two hundred friars in the Order, and many of them were doctors and theologians.[6]

*   *   *

The spiritual growth of St. Teresa is no less interesting.

6. Father Otilio, O.C.D., "St. Teresa of Avila, Mother and Lawgiver" *Spiritual Life,* (1962), 78-91.

Teresa's early childhood was characterized by astonishing religious intensity. By this the reader should
not assume that she had visions or similar unusual
privileges, as we find in the life of the Venerable Dominic of Jesus Mary or Saint Ambrose, but rather that
Teresa was, by our standards, an unusually pious
child. According to her own admission, Teresa owed
this fervor to the excellent example of her parents:
"If I had not been so wicked it would have been a
help to me that I had parents who were virtuous and
feared God, and also that the Lord granted me His
favor to make me good. My father was fond of reading good books and had some in Spanish so that his
children might read them too. These books, together
with the care which my mother took to make us say
our prayers and to lead us to be devoted to Our Lady
and to certain saints, began to awaken good desires
in me. . . . It was a help to me that I never saw my
parents inclined to anything but virtue. They themselves had many virtues."[7]

This childhood fervor gradually lessened as Teresa
grew because she surrendered to the whims of caprice.
By the time she entered her teens Teresa was spir-

7. *Autobiography,* chap. i.

itually dissipated; her psychic strength was exhausted in the pursuit of vanities, and her intellect was unable to cope with the erratic drive of her emotions. The quick action taken by her father in enrolling her in the boarding-school (when she was sixteen) had a remedial effect upon the adolescent and she repented of her frivolous, even dangerous, vanities. The conversion, however, was superficial because it did not help Teresa to master her nature. It did have one very good effect: it directed her toward the religious life.

Once the novelty of a life dedicated to God wore off, Teresa again faced a bitter strife between her emotions and her intellect. She became ill and her resultant convalescence profited her spiritual life. But, once again, Teresa devoted herself to the pursuit of vanities. The reason behind this, perhaps, was Teresa's unwillingness to face the imperfections which embarrassed her when she prayed. "The devil, beneath the guise of humility, now led me into the greatest of all possible errors. Seeing that I was so utterly lost, I began to be afraid to pray."[8] Although Teresa ne-

8. *Autobiography,* chap. vii.

glected prayer and enjoyed entertaining visitors in the convent parlor, she did encourage her father in the practice of prayer and unknowingly prepared him for a happy death. His last days on earth impressed her deeply and she sought spiritual direction from her father's confessor, Father Vincent Barron, a Dominican. From this time (1543), Teresa never again completely abandoned prayer, although she tried to compromise it with her frivolous manner of living.

When Teresa was about thirty-eight, after reading *The Confessions of Saint Augustine* and through sincere prayer for the grace of conversion, she experienced her final conversion. "It happened that, entering the oratory one day, I saw an image. . . . It represented Christ sorely wounded; and so conducive was it to devotion that when I looked at it I was deeply moved. . . . So great was my distress when I thought how ill I had repaid Him for those wounds that I felt as if my heart were breaking, and I threw myself down beside Him, shedding floods of tears and begging Him to give me strength once for all so that I might not offend Him. . . . I believe I told Him that I would not rise from that spot until He had granted me what I was beseeching of Him. And I feel sure

29

that this did me good, for from that time onward I began to improve."[9]

For the next few years Teresa was earnest in prayer and conformed her life with its demands: detachment, purity of intention, charity, humility. God rewarded Teresa by permitting her to experience the prayer of recollection, the prayer of quiet, and the first stages of the prayer of union. Her continued perseverance was rewarded by divine favors of the mystical order, culminating in her spiritual espousals with Him in 1562. At this point, Teresa was ordered to write her autobiography. The *Way of Perfection,* a practical commentary on the life of virtue, followed soon after. Then, on the morning of November 18, 1572, Teresa received an astonishing and sublime grace at Communion-time when Saint John of the Cross gave her the Sacrament: her spiritual marriage with the Son of God. "Then He revealed Himself to me . . . and He gave me His right hand, saying to me: 'Behold this nail. It is a sign that from today onward thou shalt be My bride. Until now, thou hast not merited this; but henceforth thou shalt regard My honor not only as that of thy Creator and King and God but as

9. *Autobiography,* chap. ix.

that of My own bride. My honor is thine, and thine, Mine.' "[10] A few years later she wrote her most mature work, *The Interior Castle.*

Integrity of life is a homogeneous development of the potentialities latent in an individual. This Teresa attained at her spiritual marriage for, until that time, she lacked completion ("Until now thou hast not merited this . . ."). The Saint's growth in spirituality is reflected in her books, written at different stages of that growth. Biographers and commentators often forget this. The keynote of that growth was a progressive "interiorization," particularly obvious in her description of *The Interior Castle.*

St. Teresa of Avila authored other works, but they shall not be considered in this text. Rather, our interest will center in her *Life, The Way of Perfection,* which was the apex of her ascetical teachings, and *The Interior Castle,* the climax of her mystical teachings.

Impressed by the serenity of Teresa's socratic attitude toward life and the beauty of her thought Robert Crashaw, the English poet, mused: "This is not Spanish—it is the language of heaven!"

10. *Spiritual Revelations,* No. 35.

ANALYTIC OUTLINE OF CERTAIN BASIC STAGES

Date	External Life	Writings
1515	March 28: birth in Avila, Spain.	
1521		
1528	Death of Teresa's mother.	
1531	Enrolled as a boarding-student at the convent of Our Lady of Grace in Avila.	
1536	Enters the Carmelite Order in the Incarnation convent, Avila.	
1537	Professed as a nun by taking the religious vows.	
1538	Illness; granted permission by her religious superiors to stay with her sister Maria while she took the cure; enroute she visited her uncle, Pedro.	
1540	Return to the Incarnation convent.	
1543	Death of Teresa's father.	
1554		
1556? 1558?		

IN THE LIFE OF SAINT TERESA

Psychological Development	Spiritual Life
Predominance of emotional life.	Childhood fervor.
Frivolity	Took the Blessed Virgin as mother.
Sentimental attachment to Doña Maria Brinceño; impressed by her pious example; decision to be a nun.	Repentance for her frivolity and her great fear of losing her soul.
Romantic notions of convent life.	First fervor as a nun.
Struggle to overcome emotions; nervous fatigue.	
Reads spiritual writings to Don Pedro and deeply impressed by them and by him.	Accepts illness with fortitude; her devotion to St. Joseph assumes definite form.
Return to superficial living.	Renounces practice of prayer from false notion of humility.
	Seeks spiritual direction from Vincent Barron, O.P.
Great progress toward maturity through reading Augustine's *Confessions*.	Definitive conversion; growth in prayer.
	First rapture.

ANALYTIC OUTLINE OF CERTAIN BASIC STAGES

Date	External Life	Writings
1559		
1560	In September she took the first steps toward the Reform, but it met with failure.	First spiritual relation, written to Father Pedro Ibañez, O.P.
1561		
1562	Inauguration of the Carmelite Reform by foundation of the Convent of San José in Avila, August 24th.	First draft of her *Life* and spiritual relation No. 2 to Ibañez.
1563-1565		First version of *The Way of Perfection;* spiritual relation No. 3.
1567	Founds convent at Medina del Campo; takes steps to extend Reform to the Carmelite Friars.	
1568	Founds convents in Malagon and Valladolid; with her help the friars establish a monastery in Duruelo.	
1569	Founds convents in Toledo and Pastrana.	Composes *Exclamations of the Soul to God* and the second version of *The Way of Perfection.*

IN THE LIFE OF SAINT TERESA—Continued

Psychological Development	Spiritual Life
	First intellectual vision of the Humanity of Christ on June 29th.
	Vision of Hell (*Life*, chapter 32); various visions of Humanity of Christ; makes vow of greater perfection.
	August 15; Vision in which she is assured of spiritual cleanliness (*Life*, chapter 33).
	Experiences one of the several transverberations of her heart— her spiritual espousal (*Life*, chapter 29)

ANALYTIC OUTLINE OF CERTAIN BASIC STAGES

Date	External Life	Writings
1570	Founds convent of Salamanca.	
1571	Founds convent in Alba de Tormes; from October until the October of 1574 she is prioress of the Incarnation convent in Avila.	
1572		
1573		Begins writing the *Foundations* (chapters 1-9)
1574	Founds convent in Segovia	Continues *Foundations* (chapters 10-19)
1575	Founds convents in Beas and Seville.	
1576		Completes *Foundations*, chapters 20 to 27.
1577	Great opposition to the Reform.	Composes *The Interior Castle*.
1579	Persecution abated.	
1580	Learns that Pope Gregory XIII has permitted the Reform to have its own jurisdiction; founds convents in Villanueva de la Jara and in Palencia.	Certain changes in the text of *The Interior Castle*.
1581	Founds convent in Soria.	
1582	Founds convent in Burgos; dies on October 4th in Alba de Tormes.	Makes final additions to the *Foundations*, chapters 28-31.

IN THE LIFE OF SAINT TERESA—Continued

Psychological Development	Spiritual Life
	Experiences steps preparatory to the spiritual marriage; (*Life*, chap. 39); Relations 15 & 16.
	November 18th: spiritual marriage.
	Makes vow of obedience to Father Gratian.

CHAPTER THREE

The Book of the Mercies of God

AFTER her final conversion (around 1554) Teresa advanced rapidly in the spiritual life, particularly in prayer. Because of the sublimity of these new experiences she became frightened. She feared deception and felt the need of counsel. The Jesuit Fathers had established themselves in Avila in 1554 and they enjoyed a fine reputation as confessors and spiritual guides, but Teresa considered herself unworthy to approach them with her problems, although they seemed to be the most logical to ask for direction. An acquaintance of hers was Francis Salcedo, a pious layman who had studied theology under the direction of the Dominican Order. Patiently he listened to her fears and doubts and then suggested that she contact

Father Gaspar Daza. To him she could speak more freely about the state of her soul because he was a priest. Teresa humbly followed the advice. Father Daza, although he refused to become her confessor because of his already excessive obligations, listened to her self-manifestation and made several suggestions. Because she felt that Father had mistakenly assumed her to be further advanced than she actually was, Teresa hesitated to follow his advice. . . . She returned to Salcedo. "This diligent and holy man took such pains on my behalf, that I think it was he who began my soul's salvation," recounts the Saint.

As time passed and her confidence in him grew, Teresa revealed to this gentleman the seeming contradiction between her imperfections and the sublime favors she was receiving. Salcedo became alarmed and consulted with Father Daza. Together they studied a copy of Laredo's *Ascent of Mount Sion* in which Teresa had underscored passages which seemed to her descriptive of her spiritual condition. Their conclusion was a blow to Teresa: they were convinced that she was deceived. As a remedy they suggested that she consult the Jesuit Fathers.

In preparation for the interview Teresa wrote an account of her life emphasizing the state of her soul.

Then she went to see Father Diego de Cetina. He
encouraged her by saying that she was being led by the
Spirit of God. He suggested various practical steps
Teresa could make toward greater spiritual growth.
About 1557 St. Francis Borgia visited the Jesuit
house in Avila and both Father de Cetina and Señor
Salcedo advised her to talk with him. He too approved
and offered valuable advice.

Then Father de Cetina was transferred elsewhere
and Father John de Pradanos became Teresa's spiritual director.

"This Father began to lead me towards greater perfection. He told me to leave nothing undone which
might make me entirely pleasing to God; and he
treated me with great skill, though gently at the same
time. For my soul was not at all strong, but very
sensitive, especially in respect to abandoning certain
friendships. Although these were not the cause of any
offense against God, they involved a great deal of af-
fection, and I thought that I would be ungrateful if
I were to give them up. I asked my confessor why I
must behave so ungratefully since I was committing
no sin. He told me to put the matter before God for
some days and to recite the hymn *Veni Creator* that
God might show me the better course. Having spent

a great part of one day in prayer, beseeching the Lord to help me content Him in every way, I began the hymn; and as I was reciting it a rapture came on me so suddenly that it almost carried me away; it was so plain that I could make no mistake about it. This was the first time that the Lord had granted me this grace of ecstasy, and I heard these words: *I want you to converse now not with men but with angels.* (. . .) Since that day I have had the courage to give up everything for God Who in that moment—for I think it was no more than a moment—was pleased to make His servant another person."[1]

After a couple years Father de Pradanos was also transferred. The Saint felt lost and confused. A close friend of hers, Doña Guiomar de Ulloa, suggested contacting Father Balthazar Alvarez, a young priest (only twenty-four years old) who enjoyed an outstanding reputation for his knowledge of spiritual matters.

"My confessor (. . .) was a very discreet man of great humility (. . .) he was a man of much prayer and learning (. . .) I know that he was frequently warned to be on his guard against me (Note: Teresa

1. *Autobiography,* chap. xxiv.

had been experiencing various supernatural phenomena, very suspect in those days of the Spanish Inquisition and the "purity of Faith"). Providentially he was willing to go on hearing my confessions (. . .) . He always encouraged me and quieted me (. . .) That confessor did his utmost to bring my soul to perfection (. . .) In the three and more years that he was confessing me, he endured a great deal on account of these trials of mine."[2]

When Teresa was considering the foundation of the convent of San José, she met strong opposition from various quarters in Avila. Father Pedro Ibañez, a Dominican who supported Teresa's plan, and who wrote to Rome for the first bull of authorization for the convent did a great deal to turn public opinion in her favor. He admired Teresa and asked her to write an account of her spiritual life for his study; this has since become known as the first *Spiritual Relation*. Possibly Saint Peter of Alcantara saw this manifestation. After completing his preliminary studies of Teresa's spirituality Father Ibañez requested her to write a more detailed account of her life. The Saint com-

2. Ibid., chap. xxviii.

pleted it in June, 1562, just two months before the nuns moved into the new convent.

After the furor about the convent had subsided, Father Garcia de Toledo, a friend of Ibañez and another of Teresa's confessors, suggested that the Saint enlarge her biographical account by inserting the details of the new foundation.

Father Ibañez advised Teresa to submit the manuscript to John of Avila, the saintly "Apostle of Andalucia." Obediently, the Saint entrusted the task to Father Dominic Bañez, the great Dominican theologian of the University of Salamanca. After he had read it and pronounced favorably on its contents, Bañez forwarded the manuscript to the offices of the Inquisition in Madrid. When it was returned to him without any censure of its contents, Bañez seems to have kept the manuscript for the next several years.

About this time the Inquisitor Don Francisco Soto de Salazar arrived in Avila. Teresa, alarmed by the knowledge that the autobiography was being studied by the officials of the Inquisition in Madrid, went to see him. He reassured her and suggested that she send a copy of it to John of Avila. Not personally acquainted with this priest, she prevailed upon a friend of hers, Doña Luisa de la Cerda, to give the copy to him. Time passed, but the Saint heard nothing from Andalucia. Investigation revealed that Doña Luisa had delayed forwarding the manuscript. Teresa wrote four times to urge her to complete the shipment.[3] Upon finally receiving the work, John read the text and approved it, although he suggested a few minor changes.

Meanwhile Anna de Mendoza y de la Cerda, the Princess of Eboli, heard of the autobiography and asked Teresa to permit her to read it. Teresa could not easily refuse the Princess' request; this was unfortunate. In no time, the visions, raptures, and mystical experiences described in the text were favorite conversation pieces in the drawing-rooms of the sophisticated.

Doña Anna had aided Teresa in the foundation of the convent of Pastrana. When her noble husband died, the Princess, who had a talent for the dramatic, rushed in her widow's weeds to the door of the convent and tearfully begged for admission. Teresa's wry comment afterwards was: "The Princess of Eboli as a

3. May 18, 1568; May 27, 1568; June 9, 1568; June 23, 1568.

nun was enough to make you weep.''[4] The eccentric behavior of the lady completely disrupted the convent. When she left (because she resented the prioress' authority) she revenged her hurt feelings by denouncing Teresa to the Inquisition.

Father Bañez heard of this new development and submitted the original manuscript of Teresa's autobiography along with a letter in which he expressed his favorable attitude toward it. Two theologians studied the work and expressed their approval of its contents. In order to protect it against confusion with unofficial copies in circulation, however, the authorities kept it in the Inquisition's archives. Teresa never saw it again. After the Saint's death in 1582, Anne of Jesus, one of her closest associates, obtained the release of the manuscript with permission to have it published.

II

In the prologue to the text Teresa stated the following general details about the work: (1) she wrote it in obedience to a command of her confessor and in response to a command of the Lord; (2) her purpose

4. *The Letters of St. Teresa of Jesus* (Letter 50) addressed to Father Dominic Bañez, I, 127.

was to manifest her way of life, particularly her growth in prayer (in this regard she would have liked to expose all her failings, but those in authority had put strict restrictions on this); (3) the book was intended primarily for her confessors, but she does imply that other readers are also in mind. This last statement can be substantiated from remarks made by the Saint in *The Way of Perfection.* "A few days ago (N.B.: a typical Teresian hyperbole) I was commanded to write an account of my life in which I also dealt with certain matters concerning prayer. *It may be that my confessor will not wish you to see this,* for which reason I shall set down here some of the things which I said in that book and others which may seem to me necessary"[5] "I described this as well as I was able in the relation which I made of it, as I have said, so that my confessors should see it . . . I shall not repeat myself here . . . If those of you who have experienced the happiness of being called by the Lord to this state of contemplation, *can get this book,* you will find in it points and counsels which the Lord was pleased to enable me to set down."[6] Again, in the *Book of Foundations,* Teresa remarked: "In the year

5. *Way of Perfection,* prologue.
6. *Way of Perfection,* chap. xxv.

1562, when I was in the convent of Saint Joseph at Avila . . . I was commanded by the Dominican Father Fray Garcia de Toledo, who at the time was my confessor, to write an account of the foundation of that convent, and also of many other things, *as anyone who reads the book, if it is ever published, will see.* It is now eleven years later. . . ."[7]

The epilogue, a letter written to Garcia de Toledo by Saint Teresa, corroborates the above details. She has written about "so many of my miserable deeds" and "the favors which the Lord has bestowed upon me"; she has "done what Your Reverence commanded me." She further mentions her great desire that John of Avila be permitted to see it and so be enabled to pass judgment on her spiritual life. "I am most anxious that the order shall be given for him to see it, as it was with this intention that I began to write it; and, if he thinks I am on the right road, this will be a great comfort to me. . . ."

Therefore, the book has a dual scope. At times, Teresa manifests elements from her personal life, and at other times she teaches the way of prayer.

Much difficulty has resulted from the failure of

7. *Book of Foundations,* prologue.

some to grasp the composite nature of the autobiography. Some, for example, accuse Teresa of being illogical or of disorganized thinking; others humorously refer to her "digressions" and her "typical femininity." In actuality, the book is both biographical and doctrinal; it is a compilation of a revised earlier text and a later addition. The revised original text was biographical; the addition contains doctrinal, historical, and personal elements. Readers will be aided by the following division of the chapters:

Chapters 1 to 10 —revised text—biographical
Chapters 11 to 22—later addition—doctrine of
                  prayer
Chapters 23 to 32—revised text—mainly biographi-
                  cal concerning the period after
                  her final conversation (about
                  1554)
Chapters 33 to 40—later addition—historical, per-
                  sonal elements

Generally speaking, therefore, the theme of the autobiography of Saint Teresa of Avila is the doctrine of prayer illustrated by her personal experiences. There are several minor themes: the necessity of spiritual direction, the relationship of the Humanity of Christ to the life of prayer and to the spiritual life in general, the struggle of the spirit against the devil-world combination, and the cultivation of the virtues, especially humility and fortitude.

For whom does Teresa write? To whom may it be applied? Aside from her confessors for whom she directly intended the book, Teresa had in mind a future audience composed of her Carmelites; later history has proven that all Christians can profit from it. "I shall now speak of those who are beginning to be the servants of love—for this, I think, is what we become when we resolve to follow in this way of prayer Him Who so greatly loved us."[8] In other words, Teresa addressed individuals prompted by the first stages of filial love for God to desire a more intimate relationship with Him. These are timorous individuals, however, and servile fear still dominates their outlook: "At first it causes distress, for beginners are not always sure that they have repented of their sins (though clearly they have, since they have so sincerely resolved to serve God)."[9]

III

In reflecting on the life of Saint Teresa we note a

8. *Autobiography,* chap. xi.
9. Ibid.

peculiarity of hers which sometimes dismays those who read her biography for the first time. The Saint tends to insist on her sinfulness and to classify herself with Augustine and Mary Magdalen. At the same time learned theologians tell us that she never committed a mortal sin. Did Teresa suffer from a guilt complex or from strong feelings of inferiority? That hardly seems possible given her virile stand in crisis and her logic—sometimes considered "common sense." To understand Teresa's low self-appraisal we must study her under a different light. First of all, she wrote her autobiography to manifest to her directors the state of her soul. Then, she wrote between 1562 and 1565; during this period God had blessed her with many graces indicative of a high degree of spiritual development. The nearer a person approaches God, the more aware he is of the infinite simplicity of God. In the light of that transcendent reality he sees his own spiritual integrity as deformity and complexity. The moral blemishes marring his past life seem the greatest of evils. "My Lord knows that all I desire is that He may be praised and magnified a little when men see how on a foul and stinking dunghill He has planted a garden of such sweet flowers. May it please His Majesty that I may not by my own fault root

them up again, and be once again what I was."[10]
Speaking of a vision of hell which God granted her
Teresa remarks: "I understand that the Lord wished
me to see the place that the devils had ready for me
there, and that I had earned by my sins. . . . I was terrified, and though this happened six years ago, I am
still terrified as I write; even as I sit here my natural
heat seems to be drained away by fear. . . . It is true,
I think, that my sins merited even worse punish-
ment!"[11] Thus Teresa considers herself a great sinner
and laments her failure in corresponding with divine
grace.

In the course of the centuries some have attached
revolting interpretations to the favors which God bestowed upon Saint Teresa. Pierre Cabanis (1757-
1808), the French physician and author whose liberal
views associated him with Mirabeau, called Teresa
the "patroness of the hysterical." A compatriot of his,
Henri Esquiros (1812-1876), poet, politician, and historian notorious for his socialist tendencies, is among
those who accuse the Saint of "erotomania," subject
to "amorous illusions, sexual and erotic excesses."
Alphonse Karr (1808-1890), French novelist, critic,

10. *Autobiography,* chap. xi.
11. *Autobiography,* chap. ix.

and journalist, wrote of Teresa: ". . . that Christian Sappho physically enamored of Christ, claims to have descended into hell and said that she heard the following in one of her erotic moments . . ." Emile Zola (1840-1902), famous novelist and journalist, masterful exponent of realism and champion of the Dreyfus case, attached erotic interpretations to the ecstasies of the Saint; he writes of the trembling which divine joy can put into the body of a woman, of the voluptuousness of Faith drawn to the extreme of spasm. Zola is the one who tastelessly gave an erotic interpretation to the famous statue of the "transverberation" by Bernini found in the Roman church of Santa Maria della Vittoria. A recent author has spoken of Teresa as suffering from a guilt complex, while another blithely refers to Saint Teresa's "cataleptic states." A recent translator of Teresa's autobiography has this to say of her: "Teresa seems all her life to have been overwhelmed with a sense of her own wickedness, which may have contributed to her sorry state. This habit of self-reproach, which our century has learned to think of as pathological, acts as a constant refrain in her writings. In every chapter she harps on her unworthiness."[12]

12. J. M. Cohen (trans.), *Life of Saint Teresa* (Baltimore: Penguin, 1957), introduction.

His Holiness, Pope Leo XIII, exposed the error of these and similar statements in a letter addressed to Father Bouiox, S.J., dated March 17, 1883. He wrote of her works: "They have a force more heavenly than human which rouses one marvelously to a better life, so that their reading is most profitable not only to those engaged in the direction of souls and those who tread the highest paths of virtue, but also to everyone who is at all concerned about the duties and virtues of Christian life—in other words, who is anxious about his salvation." Pope Saint Pius X's remark is also significant in this context: "Would that those who now write about what they call 'mystical psychology' would make up their minds to follow in the footsteps of this great teacher!" (March 7, 1914). No one can give what he does not possess; Teresa, with her limited scholarly background, could not have produced solid writings meriting the praise of the Sovereign Pontiffs unless she possessed a high degree of personal integrity.

Frequently, in her writings, Teresa complains of the slowness of her imagination. "My mind was so stupid that I could never call up heavenly or exalted thoughts on any occasion until the Lord had presented them to me in another way. I had so little aptitude for picturing things in my mind that, if I did not actually see a thing, I could make no use at all of my imagination in the way that others do who can induce recollection by calling up mental images. Of Christ as a man I could think, but never in such a way as to call up His picture in my mind. Although I read of His beauty and looked at pictures of Him, I was like a person who is blind or in the dark."[13] We must not take her seriously, however, because she actually had a very vivid imagination, as her writings will quickly prove. It did assume a peculiar expression in her psychological life which might justify her impatience with this faculty. As soon as Teresa possessed an image or impression of something in her phantasy, her active intellect began to work on it. It would be minutely dissected and pass quickly from the realm of generalities or dreamy images into the field of action. Teresa, therefore, did not muse long over the data presented to her intellect by the imagination. Her lack of formal knowledge of psychology accounts for her failure to understand what was happening and her impatience with her imagination.

IV

The doctrinal content of the book is devoted to a

13. *Autobiography*, chap. ix.

homely discussion of meditation. Teresa's notion of it is delightful: an intimate conversation between two lovers—the soul loving God and God loving the soul. She could not fathom anyone's hesitancy in entering this enticing relationship: "I cannot see, O my Creator, why the whole world does not strive to draw near to You in this bond of friendship. The wicked, whose nature is unlike Yours, should come to You so that You may make them good. They should allow You to be with them for some two hours every day even though they may not be with You, but are engaged in a thousand revolving thoughts and distractions, as I used to be. But by making this effort against themselves and desiring to be in such good company (. . .) every day the devil has less strength against them, till finally You give them the victory."[14]

Teresa pitied those who unwittingly increase their earthly sorrow by "closing the door on God in order to prevent His giving them the joy of prayer. I am truly sorry for them, since they are serving God at great cost to themselves. For the Lord Himself pays the costs of those who practice prayer. . . ."[15]

In order to make her explanation of prayer more palatable—since she did want to point out prayer's

14. Ibid., chap. viii.
15. Ibid, chap. viii.

charm, the Saint employed a metaphor: a garden in need of water and the four possible methods of irrigating it. The exact source of the allegory remains a mystery known only to Teresa. Twice she wrote of it and both times she said something different. Once she admitted that it did not originate with her: "I shall have to employ some kind of comparison . . . this spiritual language is so hard to use for such as, like myself, have no learning, that I shall have to seek some means of conveying my ideas. It may be that my comparison will seldom do this successfully and Your Reverence will be amused to see how stupid I am. But it comes to my mind now that I have read or heard of this comparison: as I have a bad memory, I do not know where it occurred or what it illustrated, but it satisfies me at the moment as an illustration of my own."[16] Later she remarked that its use was a usual thing with her, especially when she first began the practice of meditation: "I am pleased with this comparison, for often, when I was a beginner . . . , it used to give me great delight to think of my soul as a garden and of the Lord as walking in it."[17]

16. *Autobiography*, chap. xi.
17. *Autobiography*, chap. xiv.

The allegorical ingredients and their obvious meaning for Teresa are as follows:

the garden _____the soul
lord of the garden _____the Lord
gardener _____the soul, the rational
 faculties of man, or the Lord Himself
plants _____the life of virtue
 contained potentially in sanctifying grace
flowers _____virtues
fruit _____proven virtue
water _____various significations,
 but usually prayers and the ways of praying
irrigation _____various stages of prayer

Sometimes authors deprecate this allegory by comparing it with the one used by Saint Teresa in *The Interior Castle;* they will insist that the latter is more profound, more interior. How true it is, that comparisons are odious! One must remember that, at the time when she wrote her autobiography, Teresa had not yet attained the spiritual maturity reflected in *The Interior Castle.* Teresa's spiritual growth had blossomed into the spiritual affiance, and it was with *this* background of experience that she wrote her autobiography. Ten years filled with greater spiritual growth passed before she began her famous study of the seven "mansions" of the soul.

The Saint mentions four ways of irrigating the garden. These she arranges according to the degree of ease with which the garden is watered: by laboriously drawing water up from the well and transporting it in a bucket, by working a windlass and bucket, by enlisting the water of a stream or river, and by enjoying the gift of rain. Each of these, applied to prayer, contains a threefold division: a special grace, a particular form of prayer, and a distinct stage in spiritual growth. It must be noted that the entire exposition lacks temporal perspectives—in other words, Teresa in no way declares that a certain amount of time is required for each of these stages. Further, she does not pretend to give an exhaustive treatment of the spiritual life in these chapters; the very fact that she wrote the first version of *The Way of Perfection* during the same years in which she was revising her autobiography offers proof of the statement. "A few days ago I was commanded to write an account of my life in which I also dealt with certain matters concerning prayer. It may be that my confessor will not wish you to see this, for which reason I shall set down here some of the things which I said in that book *and others which* may also seem to me necessary."[18]

18. *Way of Perfection,* prologue.

Saint Teresa began by discussing a period in which grievous sin is more or less successfully controlled and in which the person intends to practice prayer. According to her allegory, here the gardener waters his gardens by laboriously drawing the water up from the well, only to find occasionally that the well has run dry. The Saint is describing those who apply themselves to discursive prayer or meditation although they experience fatigue and aridity from time to time.

Despite the eradication of gross mortal sin its roots remain to embarrass one in this stage by manifesting themselves. Struggling against them by coupling his talents with grace he experiences much inconstancy and yearns for the delight of spiritual consolations. He tries to recollect his faculties and remove them from the dissipated atmosphere of his past, but he finds it hard to do. "This is a very laborious proceeding, for it will fatigue them to keep their senses recollected, which is a great labor since they have been accustomed to a life of distraction . . . Beginners must accustom themselves to pay no heed to what they see or hear, and they must practice doing this during hours of prayer. . . ."[19] Sometimes beginners become so discouraged that they are strongly tempted to re-

19. Ibid.

nounce everything and to return to a more "ordinary" way of life. "What, then, will he do here who finds that for many days he experiences nothing but aridity, dislike, distaste, and so little desire to go and draw water that he would give up entirely if he did not remember that he is pleasing and serving the Lord of the garden; if he were not anxious that all his service should not be lost, to say nothing of the gain which he hopes for from the great labor of lowering the bucket so often into the well and drawing it up without water?"[20]

In describing this first stage of prayer Teresa marked two steps in it. First of all, she spoke of meditation in its stricter meaning: here the individual must depend heavily upon the activity of his intellectual faculties. He needs to consider, to reflect. The object of his meditation will vary from person to person, from time to time. "There will be many souls who derive greater benefits from other meditations than from that of the Sacred Passion. For, just as there are many mansions in Heaven, so there are many roads to them. Some people derive benefit from imagining themselves in hell; others, whom it distresses to

20. Ibid.

think of hell, from imagining themselves in heaven. Others meditate upon death. Some, who are tenderhearted, get exhausted if they keep thinking about the Passion, but they derive great comfort and benefit from considering the power and greatness of God in the creatures, and the love that He showed us, which is pictured in all things."[21]

The second step of prayer is an "acquired" contemplation, but Teresa wrote only briefly of it. Rather than have the soul fatigued through excessive consideration and probings into the mysteries of the Faith, "we must sometimes remain by His side with our minds hushed in silence. If we can, we should occupy ourselves in looking upon Him Who is looking at us; keep Him company . . . Anyone who can do this, though he may be but a beginner in prayer, will derive great benefit from it, for this kind of prayer brings many benefits; at least, so my soul has found."[22]

Teresa offers several counsels to beginners in prayer. Avoid tension and try to be natural, relaxed—Teresa could not bear melancholy saints! Beginners sometimes seem to think that, if they were to smile,

21. *Autobiography,* chap. xiii.
22. Ibid.

they would immediately destroy all recollection. Moments will come when the devil tries to discourage them through thoughts of false humility; they exaggerate their unworthiness and paralyze their entire spiritual organism. A subtle, inordinate love of the body manifests itself through fear of harming it by subjecting it to the self-discipline demanded by sincere prayer. Then, there is the immature zeal of the beginner who, only *beginning* to realize the treasure hidden in genuine spirituality, wants to make everyone extremely spiritual; Teresa fears that he will try to teach the world when he has barely enough spirituality for himself. Because there is a danger that persons in this stage of development might turn meditation-time into a study-period, the Saint counsels them to avoid excessive use of the reasoning faculties. In a more positive vein Teresa insisted upon the necessity of a spiritual director and upon docility to his instructions. As a general principle for the entire spiritual life Teresa stressed self-knowledge at every stage of development, but it must be tempered with prudence to avoid loss of time. Then, good mother that she is, Teresa recommended reading Alonso de Madrid's *The Art of Loving God,* first published in Seville in 1521.

Teresa described a second method of irrigation: "By using a device of windlass and buckets the gardener draws more water with less labor and is able to take some rest instead of being continually at work."[23] The allegory's interpretation she stated herself: "It is this method, applied to the prayer called the prayer of quiet, that I now wish to describe."

Now Teresa begins to speak of a type of prayer which borders on the "supernatural." This term assumes a special meaning in Teresian vocabulary. It refers to a divine gift which neither human industry nor diligence can acquire or procure, although one may dispose himself for it. "He sees that it is a free gift and that he can neither add to it nor subtract from it."[24] To label a state of prayer "supernatural" as Teresa understood it three qualifications must be present:

> intervention of God through a special grace
> consciousness of it either in the grace itself or in
> its effects
> a new manner of spiritual living.

The prayer of quiet understood as the second method of irrigating the garden is a gift of God and

23. *Autobiography,* chap. xiv.
24. *Spiritual Relation V,* dated 1576.

cannot be acquired, and its duration depends upon divine generosity. Teresa defined it: "This state is a recollecting of the faculties within the soul . . . the will alone is occupied in such a way that, without knowing how, it becomes captive . . . the other two faculties (i.e. intellect and memory) help the will so that it may become more and more capable of enjoying so great a blessing, though sometimes it comes about that, even when the will is in union, they hinder it exceedingly."[25] The principal activity of this state of prayer is affective. "This prayer is a little spark of true love for the Lord which He begins to enkindle in the soul." One does not become fatigued, regardless of the length of prayer, provided that God does not withdraw the grace.

Earlier we mentioned that Teresa had still not attained full spiritual maturity when she wrote her autobiography. At this point in her exposition of prayer we find an excellent illustration of our assertion. Writing of the "prayer of quiet" and the "prayer of recollection" Teresa fails to distinguish adequately between them. Only after several more years which brought greater maturity with them did the Saint

25. *Autobiography,* chap. xiv.

succeed in making a good distinction between them. This she did in *The Interior Castle*.

The effects of the prayer of quiet are growth in genuine virtue (particularly detachment), profound joy within the psyche, a sense of the nearness of God (although not always clearly perceived). A possible, but not necessary, effect of the prayer of quiet may be the gift of tears.

Teresa stressed caution for those who "grow into" this type of prayer. They can so easily be misled by a false interpretation of their spiritual state; when this happens they plunge into the pursuit of vanity and self-delusion. To help them she offered practical criteria for discerning the source of what seems to be the prayer of quiet. If it is the result of the individual's ambition—a type of nirvana—"everything is quickly over and we are left in a state of aridity," the effect, no doubt, of exhausting the mental faculties. It is diabolic in origin, "it leaves behind it disquiet and very little humility and does little to prepare the soul for the effects produced by such prayer when it comes from God. It leaves neither light in the understanding nor steadfastness in the will."[26]

26. *Autobiography,* chap. xv.

Other counsels of the Saint include a warning to ignore the caprices of the mental faculties and to be vigilant against old attachments. Spiritual direction by a *qualified* guide becomes a necessity. The individual must remain faithful to prayer and to the practice of humility.

The third method of irrigation is employment of water from a stream or river: "this irrigates the garden with much less trouble, although a certain amount is caused by the directing of it." In application, "this state is a sleep of the faculties, which are neither wholly lost nor yet can understand how they work."[27]

That Teresa emphasized the "sleep of the faculties" in her autobiography but reduced it to a mere intensification of the prayer of quiet when she wrote *The Interior Castle* should clearly indicate that the autobiography represents lesser comprehension of the development of prayer. At that later date Teresa understood far better the various stages in the evolution of prayer and their relative importance. Teresa might have suspected that she was putting too much emphasis on "the sleep of the faculties" because she remarked: "This may seem to be somewhat defen-

27. *Autobiography,* chap. xvi.

sively: just the same as the prayer of quiet of which I spoke, but it is really different—partly because in that prayer the soul would fain neither stir nor move and is rejoicing in that holy repose which belongs to Mary, while in this prayer it can also be a Martha."[28] Yet she added no new theological implications to warrant the specialized attention she gave it.

It is, of course, not an acquired state, since it is a development of the prayer of quiet. It is not the state of complete union between God and the soul. It *does* cause incomparable sweetness and delight, a "heavenly madness" in which true wisdom is acquired, and the soul is conscious of the divine activity within it. There seem to be three intensities within it and these help establish the relationship to the prayer of quiet: at first it occurs in the will alone, then it affects the will and the intellect while the memory continues to wander about, and finally the memory is captured and the total activity of the soul is immersed in contemplation and enjoyment of its divine object.

At the end of the fifteenth chapter (in which she was still speaking of the prayer of quiet) Teresa mentioned that the flowers in the garden of the soul were

28. *Autobiography,* chap. xvii.

almost ready to bloom. Now, in this stage, "the flowers are opening; see, they are beginning to send out their fragrance."[29] By flowers the Saint refers to the virtues. These first delicate moments of the flower's life are intended for the Lord of the garden alone. Later, when the divine Gardener (Teresa confused the allegory here) sends the soul water in abundance so that the appearance of the fruit is hastened, "He allows it to share the fruit with others only when it has eaten so much of it that it is strong enough not to consume it all by merely nibbling at it and not to fail to get profit from it, nor to omit to recompense Him who has bestowed it. . . ."[30] This is an interesting remark and deserves consideration by those whose task it is to form apostles, whether they be clerics, religious, or laymen; a firm grounding in prayer is an absolute necessity for effective exercise of the apostolate.

Teresa counselled souls in this state to be courageous and abandon themselves to God, allowing Him to lead them where He desires.

The fourth method of irrigating the garden is quite easy: allow Divine Providence to take care of it by

29. *Autobiography*, chap. xvi.
30. *Autobiography*, chap. xvii.

rain. This, for Teresa, signifies a state of union in which the soul is apparently passive, although it can never be completely so in this life. "All the faculties now fail and are suspended in such a way that, as I have said, it is impossible to believe that they are active."[31] The soul rejoices with incomparable peace, even though at times it is the subject of violence; it rejoices without understanding the thing in which it is rejoicing. Teresa felt that if the soul should comprehend the cause of its rejoicing it is still not in the state of union. Theology teaches that union between God and the soul occurs in the will, and from there it overflows with gladness into the intellect and the memory.

Teresa confessed an inability to explain the term "union." She was aware of her lack of technical knowledge in these matters, but she did succeed quite well in defining it from the data of common sense and experience. She said that "it is quite clear what union is—two different things becoming one."[32] Within this "oneness" there occurs an "elevation of the spirit" or "flight of the spirit" differing from union itself. The distinction here is between the *habitual state* of union

31. *Autobiography,* chap. xviii.
32. Ibid.

and the *occasional acts* which are momentary intensifications of the state. Teresa then subdivided these acts into "rapture," "elevation," "flight of the spirit," "transport," called them all "the same thing"[33] and confused them further by distinguishing various grades of these acts. The whole matter is much clearer in *The Interior Castle,* once again proving that the latter is the product of more mature thought and that the two books are not to be confused by forcing their explanations to dovetail into a synthesis.

The effects of the state of union in the soul are consoling: an awareness of the divine indwelling in the soul, a great tenderness within the soul, courage leading to real deeds of heroism, deep humility, great detachment, swift recovery in case of infidelity—in a word, spiritual maturity. "So the life of this soul continues—a troubled life, never without its crosses, but a life of great growth . . . It is God Who is the soul of that soul."[34]

33. *Autobiography,* chap. xx.
34. *Autobiography,* chap. xxi.

CHAPTER FOUR

The Way of Perfection

WHEN Teresa wrote the original *Way of Perfection,* she addressed it to the nuns in the convent of San José in Avila. These heroic women had survived the storm raised among the townspeople by the foundation of their convent and sought to devote themselves to God. Teresa established a rule to order their daily lives—a law based upon Carmelite observance in the thirteenth century when the Carmelites, newly arrived in Europe from the lands of the Middle East, had assumed the character of a mendicant Order. More was needed than a simple Rule; these zealous women wanted direction in the interpretation of that Rule, something to which they could have recourse in moments of perplexity and aridity. They asked the

Saint to write a practical commentary on their way of life.

"The Sisters of this Convent of Saint Joseph, knowing that I have had leave from Father Presentado Fray Domingo Bañes of the Order of the glorious Saint Dominic, who at present is my confessor, to write certain things about prayer. . . , have, out of their great love for me, so earnestly begged me to say something to them about this that I have resolved to obey them. I realize that the great love which they have for me may render the imperfection and the poverty of my style in what I shall say to them more acceptable than other books which are very ably written by those who have known what they are writing about. . . . My intent is to suggest a few remedies for a number of small temptations which come from the devil . . . I know that I am lacking neither in love nor in desire to do all I can to help the souls of my sisters to make great progress in the service of the Lord. It may be that this love, together with my years and the experience which I have of a number of convents, will make me more successful in writing about small matters than learned men can be. . . . I shall speak of nothing of which I have no experience, either in my life or in the observation of others, or which the Lord has not taught me in prayer."[1]

Although Teresa wrote the book for the guidance of nuns, its doctrine has a universal value and extends far beyond the cloister walls. Anyone can profit from it. In some matters adaptation from cloister life to secular life has to be made—the principles remain the same for everyone.

"Be sure that, if you do what lies in your power and prepare yourself for *high* contemplation with the perfection aforementioned, then, if He does not grant it you (and I think He will not fail to do so if you have true detachment and humility), it will be because He has laid up this joy for you so as to give it you in Heaven, and because . . . He is pleased to treat you like people who are strong and give you a cross to bear on earth. . . ."[2]

The Sisters valued this work of the Saint greatly. When she established other convents these, too, wanted copies. But the enthusiasm of the early Carmelite nuns for the book has caused a great deal of confusion during the succeeding centuries, because that enthusiasm engendered five major manuscripts

1. *Way of Perfection,* prologue.
2. Ibid., chap. xvii.

of the *Way of Perfection*. They are named after the places in which they are located: the Escorial (E), the Valladolid (V), the Toledo (T), the Salamanca (S), and the Madrid (M).

The story behind the Escorial manuscripts (i.e. the autobiography, *The Book of Foundations, The Method for Visiting the Convents,* and *The Way of Perfection*) is interesting. Well-disposed toward Saint Teresa and recipient of at least four letters from the hand of the Saint, King Philip II of Spain desired after her death to have the original manuscripts for his library in the Escorial, a structure which he had begun to build in 1562, the same year Teresa began the edifice of the Carmelite Reform in Avila. The King asked Father Nicholas of Jesus-Mary (Doria), Vicar General of the Order, to obtain copies of at least some of Teresa's works for him. By direct order Father Nicholas forced the nuns to surrender their prized manuscripts to the King. This was fortunate, because even at that early date the pages were being barbarically cut up into smaller portions to be handed out as relics! The Discalced Carmelite Order and the Catholic Church owe a tremendous debt of gratitude to this King for "rescuing" the original manuscripts.

The book, as we mentioned above, was originally

intended for the Carmelite nuns in Avila. This is the Escorial manuscript. Its general tone is one of familiarity—that of a mother writing for the guidance of her daughters. It is written in Teresa's handwriting. After the foundation of the convent in Medina del Campo (1657), the Sisters reminded Teresa of this invaluable guide to their way of life possessed by the Avila convent and asked her to allow them to have a copy also. The nuns in Avila were reluctant to part with their copy and did so only with the condition that it be returned. Saint Teresa herself rewrote the entire text, perfecting it and making it a little more universal in tone. This became the second manuscript, called the "Valladolid" copy. The Saint intended the revision to be the definitive form of the book. This version (recopied by one of the nuns, Anne of St. Peter) she sent to Don Teutonio de Braganza, the Archbishop of Evora, who wanted to sponsor an edition of it. Then an unknown "learned man" studied the text and made several "corrections" and returned it to Teresa for her approval. The Saint accepted the changes but the published edition did not appear until 1583, the year following her death. The third edition of *The Way of Perfection* is known as the "Toledo" copy. Prior to the publication of the book through Don Teutonio's influence, the nuns had made various copies of the manuscript and Teresa read them over for accuracy. Often she would make small corrections. This explains the existence of two other manuscripts, the "Salamanca" text and the "Madrid" text.

In general, the theme of the work can be summarized in the phrase "the way to the living water given by the Lord." Justification for this assertion rests in Teresa's employment of three main comparisons: "way," "water" and "teacher." "Some people . . . seem to me like (those) who are very thirsty and see water a long way off, yet, when they try to go to it, find someone . . . barring their path . . . And when, after all their labor (and the labor is tremendous) they have conquered the first of their enemies, they allow themselves to be conquered by the second. . . . Their strength has come to an end; their courage has failed them; and, though some of them are strong enough to conquer their second enemies as well as their first, when they meet the third group their strength comes to an end, though they perhaps are only a couple of steps from the fountain of living water, of which the Lord said to the Samaritan woman that whosoever drinks of it shall not thirst again. How right and how very true is that which comes from the lips of Truth Himself!"[3]

We must remember that Teresa's audience was originally composed of members of a contemplative Order. Not all of them would enjoy the full development of prayer which is contemplation, but Teresa desired each one to do everything in her power to dispose herself for it. This, then, is the great goal to which *The Way of Perfection* leads: the fount of living waters, a sublime degree of contemplation in which God and the soul are intimately united.

Divine Providence used Teresa to establish a fresh concept in religious and spiritual life: apostolic contemplation. Sixteenth century Spain has a close reresemblance to twentieth century civilization. At that time wealth from the colonies was pouring into Spain and people were able to enjoy many of the luxuries denied them during the long centuries of battle against the Moors. Like contemporary man, the Spaniard of that time had to learn to incorporate his material prosperity into his spiritual life. Teresa's efforts to return to an earlier form of Carmelite observance was not a mere return to a more intense

3. Ibid., chap. xix.

77

contemplative life; were this the truth, Teresa would have no right to special honor beyond that of other "reformers" like John Soreth and the originators of the Mantuan Carmelite Reform. Teresa was a realist: in addition to the contemplative eremitic origin of the Carmelite Order exists an indisputable fact— it is also a mendicant Order, a dimension given to the Order when it was forced to migrate into Europe through Saracen pressure in the Near East. Carmel is, therefore, an apostolic Order. The vocation of Carmel, envisioned by the Saint, is not to scorn the world but rather to work for its salvation. Contemplative life for her meant the apostolate.[4]

The first three chapters of *The Way of Perfection* explain Teresa's idea of apostolic contemplation. They give a priceless insight into her ability to grasp the significance of a reality and to draw practical conclusions from it.

The second chapter is disconcerting to the hasty reader who will dismiss it as one of Saint Teresa's

4. Excellent examples of this vocation can be found in the lives of Carmelites like John of the Cross, Thomas of Jesus, Raphael of St. Joseph, John-Vincent, Anne of Jesus, Anne of St. Bartholomew, Theresa-Margaret of the Sacred Heart, and Thérèse of the Infant Jesus.

"digressions." In it she discusses poverty. Careful reading reveals the intimate connection—in Teresian thought—between poverty and the apostolate. Poverty (or, by extension, detachment) is for the Saint a liberation to benefit the apostolate. Her insistance upon poverty seems almost excessive: "If you should do as I say and yet die of hunger, then happy are the nuns of Saint Joseph's!" "These arms (of poverty) must appear on our banners and at all costs we must keep this rule—as regards our house, our clothes, our speech, and (what is much more important) our thoughts . . . Have a care to this, for the love of God; and this I beg of you by His blood. If I may say what my conscience bids me, I should wish that, on the day when you build such edifices, they may fall down and kill you all." "But as for a large and ornate convent, with a lot of buildings—God preserve us from that! Always remember that these things will all fall down on the Day of Judgement, and who knows how soon that will be?" Teresa's purpose justifies the strong language: failure to observe poverty and detachment signified a failure to observe the Rule, resulting in the complete waste of (externally) dedicated lives.

Chapters four to fifteen discuss the moral foundation of a life dedicated to prayer. They help establish an atmosphere of total detachment and complete self-oblation, vitally necessary for spiritual growth of any kind. The sixteenth chapter seems like an epilogue or a practical conclusion to this portion, for in it the Saint discourages her nuns from accepting as a candidate anyone in whom the virtues she discussed previously are not found, at least in some stage of development. What are these virtues?

"Before speaking of the interior life—that is, of prayer—I shall speak of certain things which those who would attempt to walk along the way of prayer must of necessity practice . . . There are only three things which I will explain at some length and which are taken from our Constitution itself . . . One of these is love for each other; the second, detachment from all created things; the third, true humility, which, although I put it last, is the most important of the three and embraces all the rest."[5]

Under the heading of fraternal charity, which Teresa considers in four chapters, there is an excellent discussion of a perennial problem of persons

5. *Way of Perfection,* chap. iv.

anxious to progress in spirituality: the choice of confessors. When the Saint wrote about this problem, she wrote from long and bitter experience. While it is true that Teresa analyzes certain problems which a cloistered nun might have in dealing with a confessor, the general principles she establishes can apply to all souls. Choice of confessor and spiritual director is an important step; Teresa returns to the problem several times throughout her writings.

It is difficult to distinguish detachment and humility in *The Way of Perfection* because the author insists on their intimate relationship. In general, detachment as a topic is discussed in three chapters, and humility in four. In her treatment of humility the Saint lists several obstacles to this virtue, and she puts special stress on precedence and self-righteousness.

Chapters sixteen to twenty-six could be entitled *Prayer and Contemplation*. Two points in particular are noted: (1) a person anxious to live the life of prayer must be firmly resolved to persevere in the search for the living water; (2) mental prayer (meditation) must always be considered as a spiritual contact with the Lord.

Teresa encourages beginners in prayer. She speaks of intimacy with God with as much ease as if she were describing a conversation between herself and a close associate. She cautions against hidden pitfalls and says that the path is not an easy one; but, because it is Teresa speaking in her own inimitable way, no one will turn back from fear. Perhaps this quality of the Saint prompted the Holy Father to put the words *Mater Spiritualium* (Mother of the spiritually-minded) beneath her statue in St. Peter's basilica in Rome—for Teresa indeed is motherly.

But we must not think that Teresa is all gentleness. In her there is the same austere courage which drove the women of Avila to defend their city against marauders when their men were off to war. "You will ask why I am talking to you about virtues when you have more than enough books to teach you about them and when you want me to tell you only about contemplation. My reply is that, if you had asked me about meditation, I could have talked to you about it, and advised you all to practice it, . . . But contemplation is another matter . . . If you want me to tell you the way to attain to contemplation, do allow me to speak at some length about these things, even if at the time they do not seem to you very important, for I myself think that they are."[6] And she proceeds to emphasize humility again. "Humility is the principal virtue which must be practiced by those who pray. . . ."[7]

Humility is necessary for all. Not every one who applies himself to prayer and does it with generosity attains infused contemplation, and he needs humility. The man who does receive it needs humility in order not to distort God's gift. "I do not say this without good reason, for, as I have said, it is very important for us to realize that God does not lead us all by the same road, and perhaps she who believes herself going along the lowest of roads is the highest in the Lord's eyes. So it does not follow that, because all of us in this house practice prayer, we are all *perforce* to be contemplatives. That is impossible; and those of us who are not would be greatly discouraged if we did not grasp the truth that contemplation is something given by God, and, as it is not necessary for salvation and God does not ask it of us before He gives us our reward, we must not suppose

6. Ibid., chap. xvi.
7. Ibid., chap. xvii.

that anyone else will require it of us. . . . Let us not be discouraged, and give up prayer. . . ; for the Lord sometimes . . . gives us great rewards all at once. . . ."[8]

Teresa wants souls to persevere in prayer. She has not forgotten the more than fourteen years she could not even meditate without having a book in front of her. If God had finally rewarded her efforts, why would He not grant even more sublime graces to another soul? And even if He were not to grant these graces during one's lifetime, remember that He loved Martha and if Martha had been absorbed in devotion all the time like her sister Mary then there would have been no one to prepare the meals for Him. Teresa is a sensible woman and her advice is realistic.

In chapter twenty-six the Saint gives a method for recollecting thoughts. This is not only a very interesting chapter to read but an extremely important one. The famous Carmelite method of prayer is based upon this chapter. Followers of the Saint, especially Father John of Jesus-Mary and Father Thomas of Jesus, codified the method as an aid for novices.

At this point it might be valuable to sketch the

8. Ibid., chap. xvii.

Carmelite method of meditating; we must remember, however, that it is only a "crutch" to assist us in learning the art of prayer.

Preparatory steps:

a.) remote
negative = practice of detachment
positive = practice of the presence
of God

b.) proximate
1. examination of conscience
2. spiritual reading
3. intensification of one's
awareness of the divine
presence

Meditation Proper:
a.) representation through use of imagery
b.) reflection
c.) conversation (the *heart* of meditation)

Concluding steps:
a.) thanksgiving
b.) oblation
c.) petition
d.) prayer for assistance of the Blessed Mother

From chapter twenty-seven until the book ends with chapter forty-two Teresa writes her exposition of the *Our Father.* The prayer becomes a device which she used to explain different degrees of prayer and the sincerity which must accompany diligent application to prayer.

Special attention should be given to chapters thirty and thirty-one because in them Teresa writes about the "Prayer of Recollection." She begins by calling attention to the Divine Indwelling: "Remember how important it is for you to understand this truth—that the Lord is within us and that we should be there with Him." The Saint reflects her own life in this. Her failures in responding generously to the divine call in her earlier life resulted from unreasonable extroversion. She grew as she sought the Lord within her. A trifle impatient with those whose false humility hinders their attaining this state Teresa remarks: "Speak with Him as with a Father, a Brother, a Lord, and a Spouse—and sometimes in one way and sometimes in another He will teach you what you must do to please Him." Familiarity in this way with the Guest of the soul leads to the prayer of recollection: "It is called recollection because the soul collects together all the faculties and enters within itself to be with God." This state is an acquired one, not infused: ". . . you must understand that this is not a supernatural state[9] but depends upon our volition and that, by God's favor,

9. Cf. discussion of the Teresian "supernatural" in the preceding chapter (p. 63).

we can enter it of our own accord. . . . For this is not a silence of the faculties: it is a shutting-up of the faculties within itself by the soul." Because she experienced so many torturous doubts about the genuinity of her experiences, Teresa suggested a manner of judging the prayer of recollection: if, because of this experience, one learns to withdraw his senses from external things, if he obtains a certain degree of self-mastery, then he need not fear that he errs.

Chapters thirty-two and thirty-three treat of the prayer of quiet which "is a supernatural state and, however hard we try, we cannot reach it for ourselves; for it is a state in which the soul enters into peace, or rather in which the Lord gives it peace through His presence . . ." The prayer of quiet is the beginning of contemplation. It differs greatly from vocal prayer, under which Teresa lists the prayer of recollection. During the prayer of quiet, the will alone is held captive and the other faculties although errant, benefit from it. At times the divine communion with the will is so intense that it leaves a strong impression upon the will and one goes about the routines of daily life in a somewhat peremptory manner.

Summarizing the doctrine of *The Way of Perfec-*

tion Saint Teresa writes: "All the advice I have given you in this book has a single purpose: to lead you to give yourselves completely to your Creator, to surrender your will to His, and to organize detachment from creatures."[10]

10. Ibid., chap. xxxiv.

CHAPTER FIVE

The Interior Castle

CHRISTIAN perfection consists in the perfection of charity. "The soul is not united to God in this life through understanding, nor through enjoyment, nor through the imagination, nor through any sense whatsoever; but only through faith according to the understanding, and through hope according to the memory, and through love according to the will," wrote St. John of the Cross.[1] The theological virtues are the immediate means to union with God; through them man acts in a supernatural manner, for they have as their object God Himself. "But the greatest of these is charity"; faith and hope will not exist in the next life—they give way to vision, and

1. *Ascent of Mount Carmel,* Book 2, chap. vi.

this depends ultimately upon the conformity of the human will with the divine. "Teresa's moral ideal . . . to give ourselves completely to God—to embrace suffering—to seek God's good pleasure at all costs—to set our happiness in the will of God, even when this is repugnant to nature—is finally fully expanded in the concept of 'perfect love.' "[2] Perfect love is absolutely necessary for the attainment of spiritual perfection, and it is to this that Teresa directs souls through her immortal book *The Interior Castle.*

Teresa considered the book her masterpiece. Comparing it with her autobiography and using metaphors to avoid difficulties should the letter be intercepted the Saint said: "If Señor Carrillo (i.e. Father Gaspar de Salazar) would come here, she (Teresa herself) says he would see another (book), which, so far as she can make out, has many advantages over it, for it treats of no less a thing than the Being of God Himself (i.e. the book is purely spiritual as opposed to the personal character of the biography) . . . Its enamelling and workmanship too

2. Gabriel of St. Mary Magdalen, O.C.D., *St. Teresa of Jesus* (Westminster, Maryland: Newman Press, 1949), p. 9.

are finer, for she says that the goldsmith did not know his trade so well when he made the first jewel. The gold is also of a higher degree of purity, though the precious stones do not stand out so well as in the other. It was made by order of the Maker of the crystal (i.e. a reference to the metaphor used for the soul in *The Interior Castle*), which, they say, is very evident."[3]

Different opinions try to explain the actual genesis of the book. Some, under the leadership of Diego de Yepes, a friend of the Saint and (for a time) her confessor, claim that the book was purely supernatural in origin. De Yepes, in his biography of Teresa, claimed that Teresa had an extraordinary vision of the state of the soul both in grace and in sin and that, at the same time, she received a divine command to write the book. De Yepes prided himself on his relationship with Teresa and often asserted that she told him more than she recorded with the pen. Unfortunately, there is no substantiation for the assertion. The Prologue to the book presents serious difficulties for De Yepes' claim, for in it the Saint wrote "Few tasks which I have been commanded to

3. *The Letters of St. Teresa of Jesus* (Letter 205), addressed to Gaspar de Salazar, I, 500.

undertake by obedience have been so difficult as this present one of writing about matters pertaining to prayer." And yet there is Teresa's remark to Gaspar de Salazar in the letter quoted above: "It was made by order of the Maker of the crystal. . . ."

Others claim that the book depends upon spiritual writings of various authors. They would say, for example, that Teresa's use of the number seven to denote the several mansions within the castle establishes a definite relationship to other works of the period also employing the same number. This is too vague to merit serious consideration; even the briefest acquaintance with the Holy Scriptures will show a certain fascination with the number seven. One could remark, however, that Teresa must have recalled the novels she had read as a girl when she was searching for apt similes: the idea of the castle, a maiden in the castle, etc.

The best explanation for the genesis of *The Interior Castle* seems to be a synthesis of the two opinions. Teresa had very likely been ordered by her confessor (under the direction of Father Gratian) to write a book on the development of prayer. At first Teresa found this hard to do, as she mentioned in the Prologue, but God favored her by giving her special insights. Truths which she had been aware of previously assumed new profoundity. An illustration of this is the fact that one of the theological foundations of *The Interior Castle* is the dwelling of God within the soul. When she wrote *The Way of Perfection* ten years before, Teresa had not made as much of it.[4]

It is evident that Teresa intended this book as a doctrinal exposition, for on the back of the first page she wrote: "This treatise, called *Interior Castle,* was written by Teresa of Jesus, nun of Our Lady of Carmel, to her sisters and daughters the Discalced Carmelite nuns." Although it is immediately addressed to the Discalced Carmelite nuns, it appears that Teresa also intended it for a much wider audience: ". . . where I shall be when this is given to you to read, if, after being revised by learned men, *it is ever published.*"[5] A brief glance at the chapter headings (written by Teresa herself) will quickly convince the reader that the manner of presenting the material will benefit anyone's spiritual life.

It is amusing to note Teresa's way of insisting on the importance of the various chapters: "this chapter

4. *Way of Perfection,* chap. xxviii.
5. Remarks of Teresa in the epilogue to the book.

is profitable," "this chapter contains several good points," "should be studied with great care," "this chapter is of great profit." In fact, Teresa is so convinced of the importance of her message that practically every other chapter is indicated as profitable or meriting special study!

The imagery God employed as a means of inspiring the Saint's creativity was not new. Traces of it occur in *The Way of Perfection* (Chaps. 28 and 30). Teresa explains it in this way: "While I was beseeching Our Lord today that He would speak through me, since I could find nothing to say and had no idea how to begin to carry out the obligation laid upon me by obedience, a thought occurred to me which I will now set down, in order to have some foundation upon which to build. I began to think of the soul as if it were a castle made of a single diamond or of very clear crystal, in which there are many rooms, just as in heaven there are many mansions. . . ."[6] Greater insight revealed that in the innermost room God and the individual meet in union of love.

6. *Interior Castle,* Mansion I, chap. 1.

Through a vision Teresa saw the effect of sin upon this "crystal" of the soul: "Before passing on, I want you to consider what will be the state of this crystal, so beautiful and resplendent, this Orient pearl, this tree of life, planted in the living waters of life— namely, in God—when the soul falls into mortal sin. No thicker darkness exists, and there is nothing dark and black which is not much less so than this." "It should be noted here that it is not the spring, or the brilliant sun which is in the center of the soul, that loses its splendor and beauty, for they are always within it and nothing can take away their beauty. If a thick black cloth be placed over a crystal in the sunshine, however, it is clear that, although the sun may be shining upon it, its brightness will have no effect upon the crystal."[7]

Concrete representation of the allegory employed by the Saint is a challenge. Teresa referred to a Spanish shrub known as the "palmito." It has thick layers of leaves enclosing a succulent edible kernel. "You must not imagine these mansions as arranged in a row, one behind another, but fix your attention on

7. Ibid., Mansion I, chap. 2.

the center, the room or palace occupied by the King. Think of a palmito, which has many outer rinds surrounding the savory part within, all of which must be taken away before the center can be eaten. Just so, around this central room are many more, as there also are above it."[8]

The nucleus of the allegory is the castle, God, and the soul. In the center of the castle-soul is the "Sun," the "King," the "Palace of the King," the "apartment of the King." From this center outwards are numerous apartments signifying diverse stages of perfection and of the evolution of the prayer-life. The castle has a gate which allows entrance within—this is prayer: "As far as I can understand, the door of entry into this castle is prayer and meditation: I do not say mental prayer rather than vocal, for, if it is prayer at all, it must be accompanied by meditation."[9] Outside the gate lurk the enemies of the soul. The general allegorical element used to signify them is "reptile"; Teresa had a horror of them. She speaks of "poisonous lizards," "non-poisonous" and "poisonous snakes," and of very clever little lizards which

8. Ibid., Mansion I, chap. ii.
9. Ibid., Mansion I, chap. i.

are very hard to catch. They represent the devil and his cohorts, the attractions of the material world, and the various elements in the psychological composition of man opposing his spiritual growth. At times these creatures sneak into the lower mansions, but they are allowed to penetrate only to a certain area.

From a general consideration of these images we can understand that for Teresa spiritual growth is a gradual process of interiorization, "entering within oneself." To substantiate that we can glance at her previous life: Teresa deserted God every time that she turned "outward" to worldly vanities (novels, conversations, etc.). Each of her "conversions" meant a recapture of her faculties and a redirecting of her energies to the Guest in the center of her soul. Teresa took a long time to realize this pattern, but she understood it well when she wrote the *Interior Castle*.

The Saint employs two supplementary allegories. Fascinated by the metamorphosis of a worm into a butterfly and the new life of the latter, Teresa refers from time to time during the course of *The Interior Castle* to the silk-worm. Although the allegory belongs mostly to her explanation of the fifth mansion, she does not limit it exclusively to that mansion. The other allegory is common among spiritual writings, since it was inspired by the Holy Ghost Himself in the *Canticle of Canticles:* the matrimonial allegory.

Before considering the theological aspects of *The Interior Castle* and the main characteristics of each mansion, an important fact must be stressed. Teresa seems to prefer that we try to pass through the various mansions in order, since she suggests that "it is a very good thing . . . to begin by entering the room where humility is acquired rather than by flying off to the other rooms."[10] She does insist upon our liberty to wander through the various rooms in each of these mansions; this admonition seems intended for the guidance of spiritual directors and confessors. But the Saint was a realist and knew that God cannot be limited by a determined pattern with any given soul: "It seems that, in order to reach these (higher) Mansions, one must have lived for a long time in the others; as a rule one must have been in those which we have just described, but there is no infallible rule about it, as you must often have

10. Ibid., Mansion I, chap. ii.

heard, for the Lord gives when He wills and as He wills and to whom He wills, and, as the gifts are His own, this is doing no injustice to anyone."[11]

The theological foundation of *The Interior Castle* is therefore:

(1) the divine presence in the soul;
(2) affective union with God is the end of the spiritual life;
(3) growth in spirituality is growth in interior living.

While the first and second facts are strictly theological realities, the third combines theological and psychological elements, and Teresa describes it in the light of her own experience.

The first point, the divine presence in the soul, affords an interesting aspect of Teresian doctrine. From various remarks made throughout the course of her works we understand that Teresa learned this truth only after diligent reading and inquiry. She even mentions that several priests whom she approached about the matter could not satisfy her thirst of knowledge—something she sorely lamented, for Teresa felt that those who were to be the commanders of the walled city (which is the Church)

11. Ibid., Mansion IV, chap. i.

should be learned men, able to cope with the problems of the times.[12]

The fourth Lateran Council taught that God is everywhere through His immensity. Pope Leo XIII divided this presence of God into three equally beautiful manifestations: (1) the presence of power, by which all things are subject to Him, (2) the presence of essence, by which He is the cause of existence for all things, and (3) simple presence, by which all things are present to Him: "naked and open to His gaze."[13] All of this can be summarized by the statement that God is present everywhere through the activity of His efficient causality producing different effects in creatures. Thus theologians speak of man as the "image" of His Creator while the rest of creation bears His "imprint." Man, created in the image and likeness of God, is singled out for more grandeur, for upon that foundation is built the life of grace. God, then, is present in the soul of man, not only in virtue of His activity as Creator, but also by a personal relationship dependent upon the possession of sanctifying grace.

Teresa learned this. In the first chapter of the first

12. *Way of Perfection,* chap. iii.
13. "Divinum illud Munus," issued May 8, 1897.

mansion she says that God is present in the soul, regardless of the moral condition of the subject, through His presence of immensity. Then, in the soul possessing sanctifying grace, God resides as an active center (i.e., communicating His divine life) and as an objective center (i.e. as the object of knowledge and love).

The second point, that affective union with God is the end of the spiritual life, is expressed in many different ways: "perfection," "union with God," "end of the spiritual life." For Teresa the end of the journey is a complete union of the soul with God by transformation into Him. At that moment man can regain, within the limits imposed upon him by his infidelity in Eden, the integrity he had there. It is an affective union consisting in the full flowering of charity. The human will is subject to the Divine will in all things, and this subjection is expressed by a constant desire of glorifying God. The charity of the soul for God assumes an apostolic character. Perfect examples of this can be seen in the lives of St. Teresa Margaret and St. Thérèse of the Child Jesus, both daughters of St. Teresa.

The third point, a progressive interiorization, actually comprises a dual motion: (1) God, in the center of the soul, is dynamic and acts similar to a magnet by drawing the soul within itself to the highest level of its existence, which is its essence; there He communicates Himself to it. This is accomplished through the activity of the infused virtues centered around and guided by the theological virtues. (2) We cooperate with this divine activity through the practice of the virtues, fostered by sincere application to the prayer-life.

Objections to the *universal* validity of this process of interiorization come from persons trying to justify an apparently sound adherence to "apostolic dedication." Yet psychiatrists assert that, although interiority assumes a withdrawal from the agitation of action and general dissipation of energy, it is actually a "re-collection" of oneself and one's route in life. It is a renewal, a summation of energy for better engagement. Unless genuine interiority be found in the apostle, we can sincerely doubt the effectiveness of his apostolate.

To the Teresian notion of the "natural" belong the first three mansions; the last three fulfill her idea of the "supernatural"; the fourth mansion is a transition between the two.[14] One can imprison himself

14. Cf., chap. iii.

within the area of the "natural" through a lack of generosity or unreasonable fear. The first three mansions are "situations" of the soul, rather than "states" like the remaining four. The first mansion contains the "invitation" to prayer and the life of grace; the second includes the initial attempts to acquire the virtues; the third assumes some qualities of a "state" insofar as in it there is a somewhat ordered ascetical life with a definite form of prayer. Each mansion has its special form of prayer; progress depends upon growth in prayer and cooperation with divine grace.

The *First Mansion* is "the mansion of humility." Although one makes sincere and usually successful efforts to avoid sin, he is still deeply absorbed in the things of the world. He fears offending God and knows that he needs more "depth" to offset his dissipation. His prayer consists more or less in transitory thoughts mingled with countless distractions. The chief ascetical needs of the soul are humility and fear of the Lord. Special attention should be paid to the description of the soul in mortal sin (in the second chapter) and to that of the soul without prayer (in chapter one). The first is filled with hellish darkness; the second is paralyzed. Teresa's reflections on humility and self-knowledge, found in the second chapter, are interesting. She is quite positive in her expression: "However high a state the soul may have attained, self-knowledge is incumbent upon it, and this it will never be able to neglect even should it so desire. Humility must always be doing its work like a bee making its honey in the hive: without humility all will be lost. Still, we should remember that the bee is constantly flying about from flower to flower, and in the same way, believe me, the soul must sometimes emerge from self-knowledge and soar aloft in meditation upon the greatness and the majesty of its God. Doing this will help it to realize its own baseness better than thinking of its own nature, and it will be freer from the reptiles although the powers of resistance are increasing." To aid this strengthening process is the increased sensitivity of the human faculties toward spiritual values: "The assault which the devils now make upon the soul, in all kinds of ways, is terrible; and the soul suffers more than in the preceding mansion; for there it was deaf and dumb, or at least it could hear very little, and so it offered less resistance, like one who to a great extent has lost hope of gaining the victory. Here the understanding is keener and the faculties are more alert, while the clash of arms and the noise of cannon are so loud that the soul cannot help hearing them. For here the devils once more show the soul these vipers—that is, the things of the world—and they pretend that earthly pleasures are almost eternal . . . ."[15] Teresa warns us of a subtle temptation to seek after spiritual consolations: "Let it refrain from visiting one house after another when its own house is full of good things, if it will only enjoy them." The person has only begun to travel through the mansions, and yet he is so blind to his imperfection that he imagines he has a *right* to divine consolations. "All that the beginner in prayer has to do—and you must not forget this, for it is very important—is to labor and be resolute and prepare himself with all possible diligence to bring his will into conformity with the will of God. As I shall say later, you may be quite sure that this comprises the very greatest perfection which can be attained on the spiritual road." Persons in this mansion could profit greatly from reading *The Way of Perfection,* particularly chapters twenty to twenty-six.

Similar to the preceding two mansions and yet distinct from them because some stability has entered into the spiritual life of the subject is the *Third*

15. Ibid., Mansion II.

Mansion. He carefully avoids deliberate venial sin
and takes the novice's delight in performing pen-
ances, often those which are most convenient! He
will devote time to recollection. Thus his life is well-
ordered, but there is a danger that self-complacency
may creep in. His feeling of security in spiritual matters (actually smugness) makes him unable to understand how God could permit him to continue
experiencing aridity. This impatience only causes
more aridity. Teresa laments: "Oh, humility, humility! I do not know why I have this temptation,
but whenever I hear people making so much of their
times of aridity, I cannot help thinking that they are
somewhat lacking in it."[16] Then, too, he has a tend-
ency to preach to others, and as a remedy for this
pitfall Teresa recommends firm adherence to obedience. "What I think would be of the greatest profit
to those of us who, by the goodness of the Lord, are
in this state . . . is that they should be most studious
to render holy obedience. Even though they should
be not in a religious Order, it would be a great thing
for them to have someone to whom they could go,
as many people do, so that they might not be follow-

16. Ibid., Mansion III.

ing their own will in anything, for it is in this way that we usually do ourselves harm. They should not look for anyone cast in the same mould as themselves who always proceeds with great circumspection; they should seek a man who is completely disillusioned with the things of the world . . . Let us look at our own shortcomings and leave other people's alone; for those who live carefully ordered lives are apt to be shocked at everything and we might well learn very important lessons from the persons who shock us."[17]

When Teresa wrote, she had only the barest outline, if any, of what she intended to write. It ought not be surprising, therefore, to find that at times her treatment of the subject is confused. This is the case with the *Fourth Mansion*. According to the sequence adopted by the Saint the subject-matter of the mansion is divided into three chapters:

Chapter I: first forms of supernatural prayer in general;
Chapter II: prayer of quiet;
Chapter III: prayer of recollection and the effects of the prayer of quiet.

17. Ibid., Mansion III, chap. ii.

Actually, Teresa ought to have divided her material in the following way:

> Chapter I: general treatment of first forms of supernatural prayer;
> Chapter II: prayer of recollection;
> Chapter III: prayer of quiet and its effects.

The justification for this suggested rearrangement of Teresa's division is found in her own words beginning the third chapter of the Fourth Mansion: "First of all, I will say something (though not much, as I have dealt with it elsewhere) about another kind of prayer, *which almost invariably begins before this one.* It is a form of recollection which also seems to me supernatural . . ." That "elsewhere" is in *The Way of Perfection,* chapters twenty-eight and twenty-nine.

It will be remembered that, in her autobiography, Teresa made a great deal of the "sleep of the powers" and called it the "third water" or third manner of irrigating the garden of the soul. In discussing the fourth mansion, Teresa, much more matured in spiritual matters, mentions it only as an intensification of the prayer of quiet.[18]

18. Ibid., Mansion IV, chap. iii.

A small contradiction might distress Teresa's readers unless they are forewarned. In beginning the Fourth Mansion Teresa mentions that she will be writing about what she defines as "supernatural" states of prayer; after she completes the treatment three chapters later she admits a combination of the "natural" with the "supernatural" in the states. Perhaps the easiest manner of explaining this is the most realistic: Teresa describes a state of transition in the development of the spiritual life which borders on one side (that of the Third Mansion) on the "natural" and on the other (that of the Fifth Mansion) on the "supernatural." The prayer of recollection, which is the first form of prayer in this mansion, contains a mixture of both the "natural" and the "supernatural"; the prayer of quiet is basically "supernatural" prayer, and this is intensified in the "sleep of the powers." Teresa's own words make it quite clear. Speaking of the prayer of quiet she declares: "Let it (the soul) try, without forcing itself or causing any turmoil, to put a stop to all discursive reasoning, yet not to suspend the understanding, nor to cease from all thought, though it is well for it to remember that it is in God's presence and Who this God is. If feeling this should lead it into a state of absorption, well and good." Then, immediately after, she mentions the prayer of recollection: "With it I have included the prayer of recollection which ought to have been described first, for it comes far below the consolations of God already mentioned, and is indeed the first step toward attaining them. For in the prayer of recollection it is unnecessary to abandon meditation and the activities of the understanding."[19] In her autobiography Teresa discusses the prayer of quiet and the sleep of the powers in the second and third waters.

What is the prayer of recollection? During her treatment of the third mansion Teresa had mentioned that God at times permitted the soul to enjoy tastes of supernatural prayer which were to serve as an invitation or "enticement" to seek greater development. Then, comparing her words in *The Interior Castle* with those of *The Way of Perfection,* it seems that in the *Way* Teresa refers to a more "active" form of the prayer of recollection: "You must understand that this is not a supernatural state but depends upon our volition, and that, by God's favor, we can enter it of our own accord. . . . For this is not

19. Ibid., Mansion IV, chap. iii.

a silence of the faculties: it is a shutting-up of the faculties within itself *by the soul.*"[20] On the other hand, Teresa speaks in the fourth mansion of a "passive" prayer of recollection: "It is a form of recollection which also seems to me supernatural, for it does not involve remaining in the dark, or closing the eyes, nor is it dependent upon anything exterior."[21] Combining these two forms of prayer of recollection heightens awareness of the progressive interiorization and "supernaturalizing" of the soul so characteristic of Teresian doctrine.

The Saint insists that, although the soul may enjoy the prayer of recollection, one must be most cautious to avoid occasions of offending God, since the fall of these souls causes great damage to others.

For the transition between the prayer of recollection and the prayer of quiet Teresa has the following counsel: "Let it (the soul) try, without forcing itself or causing any turmoil, to put a stop to all discursive reasoning, yet not to suspend the understanding, nor to cease from all thought, though it is well for it to remember that it is in God's presence and Who this God is. If feeling this should lead it into a state of

20. *Way of Perfection,* chap. xxix.
21. *Interior Castle,* Mansion IV, chap. iii.

absorption, well and good; but it should not try to understand what this state is, because that is a gift bestowed upon the will."[22] The important thing, in other words, is for the soul to love much and not to think much.

What is the prayer of quiet? It might be defined as an intimate awareness of the presence of God which captivates the will and fills the body and soul with ineffable sweetness and delight. It is distinct from passive recollection, as Teresa points out by using the metaphor of water. "To understand it better, let us suppose that we are looking at two fountains, the basins of which can be filled with water . . . the water in one comes from a long distance, by means of numerous conduits and through human skill; but the other has been constructed at the very source of the water and fills without making any noise."[23] The water which is secured with so much labor refers to the prayer of recollection; the other, more easily gained, to the prayer of quiet. When the soul experiences the prayer of quiet, the consolation or joy consequent upon it is so intense and the ab-

22. Ibid., Mansion IV, chap. iii.
23. Ibid., Mansion IV, chap. ii.

sorption of the will in God so great that it flows over into the other faculties. The result of all this is a greater degree of interiority—Teresa refers to it by comparing the soul to a hedgehog or a tortoise. As counsel she suggests that when the soul does not experience the prayer of quiet it must not "stay where it is like a ninny" but employ understanding: ". . . if it did nothing more it would experience much greater aridity and the imagination would grow more restless because of the effort caused it by cessation from thought."[24]

During the writing of the *Fifth Mansion* a five month interruption occurred. At the General Chapter of the Carmelite Order held at Piacenza (Italy) in May, 1575, the General ordered Teresa to choose some convent and remain there. She left Toledo around July 17, 1577, where she had been working on this book, traveled through Madrid where she visited the convent there and finally arrived at the convent of San José in Avila. Teresa thought that she could forget about writing the book, but the precept was renewed and she resumed her writing of it. The exact point at which Teresa took up her pen

24. *Ibid.*, Mansion IV, chap. iii.

was the beginning of the fourth chapter of the Fifth Mansion.

Another interruption is discernible in Teresa's text. The third chapter treats of a form of union with God different from that about which she has been writing. It is a "natural" union in which the individual does not experience all the supernatural favors described by the Saint. In it one must strive to be fully conformed to God's will; actually, this form of union is the substantial foundation upon which the other, more dramatic, one rests: "We cannot attain to the heights I have spoken of if we are not sure that we have the union in which we resign our wills to the will of God." Firmly rooted in the love of God the individual enjoying this union can express his love in the service of his neighbor.

In discussing this mansion Teresa introduces the allegory of the butterfly. The soul is compared to a silkworm "which takes life when, through the heat which comes from the Holy Ghost, it begins to utilize the general help which God gives to us all . . ." and she limits herself to treating of the influence of prayer upon this development. The full-grown worm spins its cocoon (Christ) by renouncing self-love and self-will, by practicing detachment and by exercising the virtues. At a certain point the worm dies—this is the central point of the allegory—and the death occurs in the state of union; from it the soul emerges like a white butterfly. Afterwards, the butterfly is restless, for it knows that it cannot find fullness except in God—while, at the same time, its heart is more at peace than at any other time in its existence. In using this allegory and explaining it Teresa actually reviews the whole development of the soul.

A clear understanding of the Fifth Mansion and those which follow it demands an explanation of Teresa's idea of union. Equating perfection and union Teresa remarks that spiritual perfection consists in a union of conformity between the human will and the divine will which is so all-embracing that all the faculties and aspirations of the soul must be directed to it. In commenting upon the union the Saint does not consider special extraordinary favors: her concern is with the fundamental notion of union mentioned above. Yet, from her writings, a threefold division of union is possible: (1) *substantial union,* which exists between the Creator and His creature in virtue of which He maintains the creature of existence; (2) *"natural" union,* obtained by the soul by cooperating with the divine grace but without the presence of extraordinary (or "supernatural") favors; (3) *"supernatural" union,* discussed in the Fifth Mansion. In this state the Lord draws the soul into its center where He communicates with it in its essence and holds all its faculties in His hand. It began in a very primitive stage in the fourth mansion by a certain degree of union in the will; in the fifth mansion it developed into union within the essence of the individual; in the remaining two mansions it becomes ever more intensified, until it *seems* to equate the union with God possible only in heaven. In the fifth mansion, wherein union is still in its earlier stages, the individual tends to err by excessive zeal for the glory of God and to become disturbed thereby.[25]

In general, then, St. Teresa writes in the fifth mansion about the first *purely* supernatural state of the soul in which it experiences union with God. One is aware of the presence of God but fears his own weakness. There is evidence of a sincere understanding of the apostolate: one realizes that his interior life can be of value to the Church, regardless of whether or not he is allowed to perform the external acts of the apostolate.

25. Ibid., Mansion V, chap. ii.

Teresa's discussion of the *Sixth Mansion* centers around mystical phenomena. The soul slowly becomes acclimatized to its sublime relationship with God and is being prepared for the spiritual marriage of the seventh mansion. At first the divine communication to the soul is more intense than the human faculties can bear, but the situation becomes less dramatic as the soul begins to feel more at home in this nearness to God, and the body accepts the spiritual dominion of the soul. In the seventh mansion there will be no more violence; that is the characteristic of the sixth mansion.

The various phenomena about which Teresa talks can be listed under several headings: (1) sudden calls "like thunder"; (2) sudden inflammations of the will; (3) locutions; (4) rapture, ecstasy, and transports; (5) visions. Does the Saint consider these essential to the perfection of the spiritual life? No, in view of certain facts:

(1) she wrote from an empirical point of view and so wrote from her own experience;

(2) she did not deny the efficacy of the phenomena (Mansion VI, chapter 4) but she remarked that "we must base our judgments on the virtues" (ibid. chapter 8);

(3) she gave reasons why these phenomena were not to be desired (ibid. chapter 9);

(4) she did admit, however, that they could assist in the attainment of the virtues; at the same time she insisted that virtues attained in the darkness of Faith (to borrow a phrase from St. John of the Cross) are greater and more meritorious (ibid. chapter 9).

Despite the "delights of this mansion the individual faces serious trials, for he is still undergoing the process of purification: (1) he suffers from the persecution of acquaintances who cannot understand him; (2) he must undergo physical torments, sometimes in the form of intense, passionate desires for closer union with God which seem completely frustrated; (3) he suffers from interior torments, usually in the form of fearing self-delusion and being unable to find a confessor or director who understands the state of his soul; (4) the devil too will afflict him by sundry torments.

An outstanding characteristic of St. Teresa is her intense devotion to the Sacred Humanity of the Redeemer. In her treatment of this mansion she is careful to affirm the position of the Humanity despite the lofty development of the soul: "The last thing we should do is to withdraw of set purpose from our greatest help and blessing, which is the most Sacred Humanity of Our Lord Jesus Christ."[26] Teresa felt that neglect of the Humanity of Christ was a sure sign that the soul would never enter the sixth or seventh mansion. She did admit, however, that the soul *could* lose sight of it during the act of contemplation, but she mentioned that she could not understand how this was done. Yet "I think I have explained what it is well for you to know— namely, that however spiritual you are, you must not flee so completely from temporal things as to think that meditation on the Sacred Humanity can actually harm you."

Before considering the *Seventh Mansion* attention must be called to Teresa's use of the matrimonial symbolism in speaking of the relationship between God and the soul. In the fifth mansion, where the union of the soul with God is experienced in a transitory way, Teresa appears to speak about "visits" between the two lovers. In the sixth mansion Teresa definitely speaks of the "spiritual espousal" which might be defined as "the promise of God to soon elevate the soul to perfect union or, in other words, to

26. Ibid., Mansion VI, chap. vii.

the spiritual marriage." In this sixth mansion God shows the soul His desire of being closely united with it, and the vehemence of His desire is obvious through the phenomena which overpower the human faculties. It is in the seventh mansion that the soul is elevated to the "spiritual marriage."

The Lord Himself introduces the soul into the mansion by "an intellectual vision in which, by a representation of the truth in a particular way, the most Holy Trinity reveals itself, in all three Persons . . ."[27] The mansion is located in the center of the soul where God dwells. Because of this one becomes overpoweringly aware of the indwelling of the Holy Trinity. He first experiences this in a particularly convincing way through an introductory vision; after that, the indwelling might not be as clearly delineated, but he is aware of this companionship. Further growth in charity is posssible: "It seems that the Divine Majesty, by means of this wonderful companionship, is desirous of preparing the soul for yet more. For clearly she will be assisted to go onward in perfection . . ."[28] A peculiar phenomenon is mentioned by Teresa with reference to this mansion; in

27. Ibid., Mansion VII, chap. i.
28. Ibid., Mansion VII, chap. i.

doing it she is forced to use terminology unfamiliar
to her. She speaks of a cleavage within the "soul":
"So in a sense she felt that her soul was divided; and
when she was going through great trials, shortly after
God had granted her this favor, she complained of
her soul, just as Martha complained of Mary. Sometimes she would say that it was doing nothing but
enjoying itself in that quietness, while she herself
was left with all her trials and occupations so that
she could not keep it company . . . Although of
course the soul is not really divided, what I have said
is not fancy, but a very common experience. . . . So
subtle is the division perceptible between them that
sometimes the operation of the one seems as different
from that of the other as are the respective joys that
the Lord is pleased to give them."[29] The Saint cannot express herself with technical precision, but her
description evidences her psychological genius. The
higher portion of the soul experiences a habitual
state of contemplation as opposed to the acts of contemplation it previously enjoyed; the lower portion,
or that which involves the functioning of the faculties, must face the demands of daily living; hence the

29. Ibid., Mansion VII, chap. i.

apparent—but not real—cleavage within the soul. Actually, the serenity engendered within the soul's communication with God in the affective union of wills overflows into the decisions which affect one's course of action. Obviously, a form of the apostolate will be involved in this, for the intense love experienced by the soul makes it concentrate "upon finding ways to please Him and upon showing Him how it loves Him."[30] Love must diffuse itself through activity; it demands expression.

The spiritual marriage comes about through an imaginary vision of the Sacred Humanity, very different from any preceding vision, by which the soul recognizes the sublimity of what the Lord is doing to it. In Teresa's own life it was affected by a vision wherein the Lord handed her a symbolic nail and remarked: "It is a sign that from today onward thou shalt be My bride."[31] For Catherine of Sienna it was done by the Christ Child's slipping a ring upon her finger. This vision occurs within the essence of the soul. This is to be expected, since the spiritual marriage in all its sublimity takes place at the highest point of an individual's human nature: within his

30. Ibid., Mansion VII, chap. iv.
31. *Relation* XXXV.

essence. Teresa experienced great difficulty in trying to explain or to describe the communication or the joy resulting from it, for the experience is ineffable. "Perhaps when St. Paul says: 'He who is joined to God becomes one spirit with Him,' he is referring to this sovereign marriage, which presupposes the entrance of His Majesty into the soul by union. And he also says: 'For me to live is Christ, and to die is gain.' This, I think, the soul may say here, for it is here that the little butterfly to which we have referred dies, and with the greatest joy, because Christ is now its life."[32]

32. *Interior Castle,* Mansion VII, chap. ii.

CHAPTER SIX

A Teresian Bibliography

(English Authors or Translated Works)

Bibliographies

Benno of St. Joseph, O.C.D. "Bibliographia Carmelitana Recentior (1946-1949)," *Ephemerides Carmeliticae,* I (1947), 393-416; II (1948), 561-610; III (1949), 139-219.

Curzon, Henri de. *Bibliographie Thérèsienne.* Ouvrages français et étrangers sur Sainte Thérèse et sur ses oeuvres. Bibliographie critique. Paris: Librarie des S-P., 1902.

Jiminez-Salas, Maria. *Santa Teresa de Jesús: Bibliografía Fundamental.* Madrid: C.S.I.C., 1962.

Otilio del N.J., O.C.D. *Bibliografía Teresiana.* Obras Completas de Sta. Teresa de Jesús. Madrid: Biblioteca de Autores Cristianos (BAC), 1951, t. I., pp. 23-127.

Simeon of the Holy Family, O.C.D. "Bibliographia Carmeli Teresiani," in the various issues of *Archivum Bibliographicum Carmelitanum,* published as a supplement to *Ephemerides Carmeliticae.*

Valenti, José Ignacio. *Estudio crítico-bibliográfico sobre las obras de Santa Teresa de Jesús,* Reus: Tip. Sanjuán Hnos, 1916.

Biographies

Auclair, M. *Teresa of Avila.* Preface by André Maurois. Translated by Kathleen Pond. New York: Pantheon Books, Inc., 1953.

Barden, M. H. "Saint Teresa Mirrored in Her Letters," *Thought,* VII (1932-1933), 225-239.

Beevers, J. *St. Teresa of Avila.* New York: Doubleday and Co., Inc., 1961.

Bertrand, L. *Saint Teresa of Avila.* Translated by Marie Louise Hazard. New York: The Society of the Propagation of the Faith, 1929.

Breen, P. *Compendious Critical Life of St. Teresa.* 1946.

Brice, C. P. *Teresa, John and Therese.* A family portrait of three great Carmelites: Teresa of Avila, John of the Cross, and Therese of Lisieux. New York: Fr. Pustet, 1946.

Bruno of Jesus Mary, O.C.D. *Three Mystics: El Greco, St. John of the Cross and St. Teresa.* Ed. Father Bruno of Jesus Mary, O.C.D. New York: Sheed and Ward, circa 1947.

Burton, D. "The Star of Carmel: St. Teresa of Avila," *The Girl's Book of Saints.* London: Sands and Co., 1958. Pp. 30-44.

Butler, Alban. *The Life of St. Teresa, Foundress of the Reformation of the Barefoot Carmelites.* Dublin, J. Duffy and Co.

Byron, M. *Saint Teresa of Avila.* ("Golden Hours with the Saints.") London: Hodder.

Carmelite Nun. "Woman or Saint," *Ave Maria,* 97 (1963) 8-10.

Carmel of Wheeling, West Virginia. See below under "Mary Magdalen."

Castro, Albarrán A. de. *The Dust From Her Sandals.* Reminiscences of St. Teresa of Avila. New York: Benziger Bros., 1936.

Chesterton, C. *Saint Teresa.* London: Hodder.

Carmichael, M. "Saint Teresa and her Prior General," *Thought,* VII (1932-1933), 240-261.

Coulson, J. *The Saints.* A concise biographical dictionary. London: Burnes and Oates, 1958.

Crisogono, Father, O.C.D. *Saint Teresa of Jesus:* Her Life and her ascetico-mystical doctrine. Adapted by Father Stanislaus of Jesus, O.C.D. India: Alwaye, 1939.

Cunningham, Graham G. *Saint Teresa:* An account of her life and times, including portions from the history of the last great Reform among the Religious Orders. 2 vols. London: Adam and Charles Black, 1894; 2nd ed. London: Eveleigh Nask, 1907.

Fülöp-Miller, R. *Saints That Moved the World:* Anthony, Augustine, Francis, Ignatius, Theresa. Translated by Alexander Gode and Erika Fülöp-Miller. New York: Thomas Y. Crowell Co., 1949.

Gabriel of St. Mary Magdalen, O.C.D. *Saint Teresa of Jesus.* Translated by a Benedictine of Stanbrook Abbey. Westminster, Md.: The Newman Press, 1949.

Gilman, F. G. *Saint Teresa of Avila,* 1889.

Hamilton, Elizabeth. *The Great Teresa.* London: The Catholic Book Club, 1960.

———. *Saint Teresa: A Journey to Spain.* New York: Charles Scribner's Sons, 1959.

Hester, H. C. *Saint Teresa of Spain.* London: Methuen and Co., 1909; 2nd ed. 1910.

Homan, H. W. "Saint Teresa of Avila," *Sign,* 38 (1959), 17-19.

Goodier, A. "St. Teresa and the Dominicans," *Month,* 163 (1936), 247-257.

———. "St. Teresa and the Society of Jesus," *Month,* 163 (1936), 395-405.

Joly, H. *Saint Teresa.* Translated by Emily M. Waller. London: 1903.

Kelly, J. *Meet Saint Teresa.* An introduction to "La Madre" of Avila. New York: Fr. Pustet Co., 1958.

Kennedy, M. M. *The Holy Child Seen by Saint Teresa.* Illus. Lindsay Smygnton. London: Burnes & Oates Ltd., 1913.

Keyes, Frances P. *Land of Stones and Saints.* New York: Hawthorn, 1957.

Knowles, David. *Introduction to the Life of Saint Teresa.* Translated by D. Lewis. Westminster, Md.: The Newman Press, 1962.

Lewis, D. *Saint Teresa.* London: Catholic Truth Society, 1958. Illustrated.

Life of Saint Teresa. Abridged from her own writings. London: 1757.

Lockhart, E. (ed.) *The Life of Saint Teresa of the Order of Our Lady of Mount Carmel.* With a preface by the Archbishop of Westminster, Cardinal Manning. London.

Lovat, A. (tr.) *The Life of Saint Teresa.* With a preface by Msgr. Robert Hugh Benson. London: 1911; 2nd ed. 1914.

Marie-Joseph, F., O.C.D. *Popular Life of Saint Teresa.* Translated by Anne Porter. New York: Benziger Bros., 1884.

Martin, John. "Theresa of Avila, Finest Flower of Spain's Golden Age," *The Catholic Messenger* (diocesan paper, Davenport, Iowa), 81 (1963), 11.

Mary Magdalene of Jesus (Potts), O.C.D. *Saint Teresa of Jesus*. Wheeling, West Virginia: The Carmel of Wheeling, 1914.

Matheson, Charles. "Saint Teresa of Avila: A visit to the home of Carmel's great mystic," *Mary*, XVII (1956), n. 5, 21-23.

Mullahey, K. *Teresa of Avila: The Woman*. New York: Fr. Pustet, 1929.

Nevin, Winifred. *Heirs of St. Teresa of Avila*. Milwaukee: Bruce, 1959.

———. *Teresa of Avila*. Milwaukee: Bruce, 1956.

Nigg, W. *Great Saints*. Translated by W. Stirling. 1948.

———. *Warriors of God*. The great religious orders and their founders. Translated by Mary Ilford. New York: A. Knopf, 1959. Cf. "Saint Teresa and Carmel," pp. 280-314.

O'Brien, Kate. "Salute to Saint Teresa," *Woman's Journal* (1946); condensed in *The Catholic Digest*, X, (1946), 35-38.

———. *Teresa of Avila*. New York: Sheed and Ward, 1951.

O'Faolain, Sean. *Saint Teresa and Other Stories*. London: J. Cape, 1947.

Osgood, M. *Saint Teresa and the Devotes of Spain*. Boston, 1849.

Papásogli, Giorgio. *St. Teresa of Avila*. Translated by G. Anzilotti. New York: Society of St. Paul, 1958.

Peers, E. Allison. *Handbook to the Life and Times of St. Teresa and St. John of the Cross*. Westminster, Md.: The Newman Press, 1954.

———. *Mother of Carmel*. New York: Morehouse-Gorham, 1946.

———. *Saint Teresa de Jesús and Other Essays and Addresses*. London: Faber and Faber, 1953.

———. *Studies of the Spanish Mystics.* 2 vols. New York: The Macmillan Co., 1951.

Pius X. *Apostolic Letter dated March 17, 1914.* Wheeling: Carmel of Wheeling, 1915.

Sackville-West, V. *The Eagle and the Dove.* A study in contrasts: St. Teresa of Avila and St. Therese of Lisieux. New York: Doubleday and Co., 1944.

Silverio de Santa Teresa, O.C.D. *Saint Teresa of Jesus.* Translated by Sister Teresa of the Heart of Jesus. London: Sands and Co., 1947. (distr. in the United States by Newman Press, Westminster, Md.)

Sheed, Frank J. *Saints are not Sad.* Forty biographical portraits. New York: Sheed and Ward, 1949. (Cf. pp. 334 sq. for St. Teresa.)

Sisters of Notre Dame. *Saint Teresa and Her First English Daughters.* London: Sands and Co., 1919. Illustrated.

Swainson, W. P. *Teresa of Avila.* ("Christian Mystics.") London: 1903.

Trench, M. *The Life of St. Teresa.* London: 1875.

Walker, Helen. "My Favorite Saint: Saint Teresa of Avila," *Sign,* 38 (1939), n. 11, 17-19.

Walsh, William T. *Saint Teresa of Avila.* Milwaukee: Bruce, 1943.

Windeat, M. Fabian. *Saint Teresa of Avila Coloring Book.* Illus. G. Harmon. Saint Meinrad, Ind.: Grail, 1955.

Windham, J. *Six O'Clock Saints.* Illus. M. Doneux. London: Sheed and Ward, 1954.

Wortham, H. E. *Three Women: St. Teresa, Mme. Choiseul, Mrs. Eddy.* Boston: Brown and Co., 1930. (Cf. pp. 1-114 for "Saint Teresa and the Ideal.")

Whyte, Rev. Dr. A. *Santa Teresa: An Appreciation.* 1st ed. Edinburgh: 1897; 2nd ed. New York: 1899.

Studies

Abasolo, Msgr. (Father Ambrosio, O.C.D.). "Saint Teresa and Priests," *Eucharist and the Priest,* 68 (1962) 259-270.

Aloysia, M., O.F.M. "Living the Lord's Prayer According to St. Teresa of Avila," *Mary,* XVII (1956), 24-29.

Alphonsus of the Mother of Sorrows, O.C.D. *Practice of Mental Prayer and Perfection.* 6 vols. Based upon the doctrine of St. Teresa. Translated by Rev. Jerome O'Connell, O.C.D. Bruges-Rome: Desclee de Brouwer, 1910.

Augustine, Fr., O.C.D. "Glorious Father," St. Teresa's Devotion to St. Joseph, *Spiritual Life,* VIII (1962), 120-124.

Benedict of the Mother of God, O.D.C. "The Way of Perfection," *Mount Carmel,* 8 (1960), 16-25.

Brandsma, Titus, O. Carm. *Carmelite Mysticism—Historical Sketches.* Chicago: The Carmelite Press, 1936.

Braybrooke, Neville. "Celestial Castles." An approach to St. Theresa and Franz Kafka, *Dublin Review,* 229 (1956), 427-445. Reproduced in *Spiritual Life,* III (1957), 46-56.

———. "The Flaming Heart: A Dialogue for Two Voices," *Aylesford Review,* 3 (1960), 3-9.

———. "The Geography of the Soul: St. Teresa and Kafka," *The Dalhouse Review,* 38 (1958), 324-330.

———. "St. Teresa of Avila," *Spiritual Life,* VII (1961), 253-260.

———. "Within the Soul: Teresa of Avila and Franz Kafka," *Renascence,* 13 (1960), 26-32.

Britto, John, C.M.I. "Saint Teresa and Oriental Spirituality," *Eucharist and Priest,* 68 (1962), 291-302.

Broderick, James, S.J. "St. Teresa's Drum," *The Month,* 185 (1948), 109-113.

A Teresian Bibliography

Buckley, Senam, O.C.D. "Saint Teresa in Her Writings," *Eucharist and Priest,* 68 (1962), 303-311.

Carmelo de Jesus Maria, O.C.D. "The Missionary Spirit of Saint Teresa," *Charitas,* V (1937), 19-24.

Cassidy, J. F. "The Common Sense of St. Teresa of Avila," *Irish Ecclesiastical Record,* 41 (1933), 128-135.

Conway, E. C. *More Little Ways.* 1st ed. London: Burnes and Oates, 1959; 2nd ed. Baltimore: Helicon, 1960.

Dohan, D. "St. Teresa and Common Sense," *Spiritual Life,* V (1959), 218-225.

Doheny, J. *The Pater Noster of St. Teresa.* A commentary on the *Lord's Prayer.* Milwaukee: Bruce, 1942.

Elguera, A. "The Legacy of Saint Teresa," *Commonweal,* 77 (1962), n. 11, 271-273.

Elliot, W., C.S.P. "A Patroness for Missionaries," *The Church Calendar of West Virginia,* 26 (1932), 5.

Farges, Msgr. Albert. *Mystical Phenomena.* A treatise on Mystical Theology according to the principles of St. Teresa. London: Burns, Oates and Washbourne, 1926.

———. *The Ordinary Ways of the Spiritual Life.* A treatise on Ascetic Theology according to the principles of St. Teresa. London: Burns, Oates and Washbourne, 1927.

Frassinetti, G. *Saint Teresa's Pater Noster.* Translated by William Hutch. New York: Benziger Bros., 1887.

Gabriel of St. Mary Magdalen, O.C.D. "Characteristics of Teresian Spirituality," *Spiritual Life,* I (1955), 38-55.

———. *Saint Teresa of Jesus: Mistress of the Spiritual Life.* Translated by a Benedictine of Stanbrook Abbey. Cork: The Mercier Press, 1949.

Graef, Hilda. *The Light and the Rainbow.* Westminster, Md.: The Newman Press, 1959. (Cf. pp. 310-352: "The Carmelites: St. Teresa of Avila, St. John of the Cross.")

———. "The Uniqueness of St. Teresa," *Mount Carmel,* X, 49-52.

Gray, C. *Visions of St. Teresa.* Chicago: 1900.

Hinnebusch, Paul, O.P. "The Prayer of Remembering According to St. Teresa of Avila," *Cross and Crown,* 11 (1959), 174-179.

Hoornaert, R. *Saint Teresa in Her Writings.* Translated by Rev. J. Leonard, C.M. New York: Benziger Bros., 1931.

Hough, Mary E. *Saint Teresa in America.* New York: Hispanic Institute, 1938.

Kaiser, A. "Saint Teresa's Hymn in the Light of her Autobiography," *The Ecclesiastical Review,* 91 (1934), 159-169.

Knowles, David. "Contemplative Prayer in Saint Teresa," *Downside Review,* 51 (1933).

Lavelle, Louis. *The Meaning of Holiness.* New York: Pantheon Books, 1954. (Cf. pp. 71-92 "Saint Teresa: The Union of Contemplation and Action.")

Lea, C. H. *Chapters From the Religious History of Spain Connected with the Inquisition.* Philadelphia: 1890.

Lepee, Michael. "Saint Teresa of Jesus and the Devil," *Satan.* New York: Sheed and Ward, 1952. Pp. 97-102.

Long, T. K., C.Ss.R. "Saint Teresa of Avila: Saint Alphonsus' Second Mother," *Eucharist and Priest,* 68 (1962), 312-317.

Lucas de San Jose, O.C.D. *Saint Teresa's Book Mark.* A meditative Commentary. Translated by a Friend of the Carmel of St. Louis. St. Louis: H. S. Collins Printing Co., 1919.

Luke of St. Mary, O.C.D. *Letter to the Order of the Discalced Carmelites.* Translated by the Carmel of Santa Clara, 1922.

Marie-Eugene de l'Enfant Jesus, O.C.D. *I Want to See God.* Volume I. A practical synthesis of Carmelite spirituality, based upon the *Interior Castle* of St. Teresa. 2 vols. Translated by Sister M. Verda Clare, C.S.C. Notre Dame, Indiana.

————. *I Am A Daughter of the Church.* Volume II. A practical synthesis of Carmelite spirituality, based upon the *Interior Castle* of St. Teresa. 2 vols. Translated by Sister M. Verda Clare, C.S.C. Notre Dame, Indiana: Fides Pbl. Assoc. 1955.

Mary of the Blessed Sacrament, O.C.D. *A Retreat under the Guidance of St. Teresa.* Prefaced by a letter of commendation by Cardinal Mercier. London: Burns and Oates, 1929.

Maw, M. B. *Buddhist Mysticism.* A study based upon a comparison with the mysticism of St. Teresa and Juliana of Norwich. Bordeaux: Cambette, 1924.

Melo, Carlos, S.J. "Saint Teresa and the Blessed Sacrament," *Eucharist and Priest,* 68 (1962), 331-335.

Michael Angel, Father, O.C.D. "St. Teresa, Mater Spiritualium," *Mount Carmel,* X, 63-68.

Michael, Father, O.D.C. "St. Teresa, Mater Spiritualium," *Mount Carmel,* X, 63-68.

Monica, M., O.C.D. "A Strange True Story of Teresa of Jesus," *Placidian,* V (1928), 26-29.

Norbert of the Blessed Sacrament, O.D.C. "The Holy Mother Solves a Problem," *Mount Carmel,* X (1962-1963), 77-80.

————. "Saint Teresa the Missionary," *Mount Carmel,* VII (1959-1960), 57-59.

Otilio del Niño Jesus, O.C.D. "The Marian Spirit of Saint Teresa of Jesus," *Mount Carmel,* Vol. XXII (1942).

————. "Saint Teresa of Avila, Mother and Lawgiver," *Spiritual Life,* VIII (1962), 78-91.

Pascal of the Blessed Sacrament, O.C.D. "A Visual Aid to the Interior Castle," *Ephemerides Carmeliticae,* 13 (1962), 566-575.

Pond, Kathleen. "The Influence of Other Writers on St. Teresa," *Mount Carmel,* X (1962-1963), 81-85.

Rivet, Mother Majella. *The Influence of the Spanish Mystics on the Works of Saint Francis de Sales.* Washington: Catholic University Press, 1941.

Robilliard, J. A., O.P. "An Introduction to the Interior Castle," *Cross and Crown,* XIII (1961), 438-453.

Rohrbach, Peter-Thomas, O.C.D. *Conversation with Christ.* An introduction to mental prayer, based upon the Teresian Writings. Notre Dame, Indiana: Fides Pbl. Assoc., 1956.

———. "Saint Teresa's Method of Meditation," *Spiritual Life,* I (1955), 94-99.

Snyder, Isabel. "Saint Teresa Goes on the Stage," *The Parish Visitor,* 27 (1951), n. 8, 41-48; n. 9, 34-40.

Teresa Margaret, Sister, D.C. "Way of Perfection," *Mount Carmel,* X. (1962-1963), 69-76.

Thomas of the Cross, O.C.D. "From St. Teresa to St. Joseph," *Mount Carmel,* X (1962-1963), 53-62.

Literature

Clarke, W. F., S.J. "Martyr of Love (a poem)," *The Church Calendar of West Virginia,* 26 (1922), 6-7.

Crashaw, Richard. *Poems of St. Teresa.* Ed. Leonard Martin. New York: Oxford Press, 1927.

Keenan, Cecile Joyce. "The Pride of Spain (a poem)," *The Church Calendar of West Virginia,* 26 (1922), 3-4.

Waggaman, Mary T. "To Saint Teresa of Jesus (a poem)," *The Church Calendar of West Virginia,* 26 (1922), 2.

Sermons and Devotions

Alexis of St. Joseph, O.C.D. *A Novena to the Seraphic Mother Saint Teresa of Jesus.* Translated by Peregrinus. New Orleans: M. F. Dunn and Bros., 1882.

Balfe, K. M. *Thoughts of St. Teresa for Every Day*, 1925.

Bossuet, Jean-Jacques. "Panegyrie of St. Teresa," *Panegyrics of the Saints*, ed. Rev. Dr. O'Mahony. London: B. Herder Co., 1924. Pp. 130-147.

Carmel of Buffalo. *Saint Teresa of Jesus, Spiritual Mother*. Buffalo: 1962.

Carmel of New York. *Novena to St. Teresa of Avila in Thanksgiving for Peace*. New York: 1945.

Heuser, H. *Repertorium Oratoris Sacri*. 6 vols. New York: Fr. Pustet, 1894. (Cf. Vol. IV, pp. 451-455: "The Sanctity of St. Teresa.")

Liguori, St. Alphonsus. *A Novena in honor of St. Teresa*. With a preface by Cardinal Gibbons. Philadelphia: McManus Press, 1914.

Mary Magdalen of Jesus (Potts), O.C.D. *Devotions in Honor of St. Teresa*. Wheeling, West Virginia: Carmel of Wheeling, 1922.

DATE DUE

MY 2 '88			
NOV 29 1993			
SEP 22			
GAYLORD			PRINTED IN U.S.A.